CW01511728

TRUTH

From the Top Down

**Writings of David Phare
Enlightened Mind and Avatar
Teacher of *A Course In Miracles***

Copyright © 2016 David Phare

All rights are reserved. The material contained within this book is protected by copyright law, no part may be copied, reproduced, presented, stored, communicated or transmitted in any form by any means without prior written permission.

ISBN: 9780646955025   eISBN: 9780646955056

INTRODUCTIONS

I produce this little book solely for YOU.

It is an attempt to impart some of the leanings of my lifetime of spiritual pursuit so you may find peace on your journey through this world of duality and death.

It is not meant to be easily understood, nor is it deliberately made difficult. This is the only way I can put such material together, it has no beginning, middle or end.

It is a compilation of writings that have accumulated over the last 19 years, a journal of sorts if you like.

If this book helps you FANTASTIC, if not FANTASTIC too! I All things are meant to be; as you will discover (despite arguments) as you go along!

Your ignorance about life's meaning, place in the universe(s), the emptiness you feel that causes you to search for peace and love in 'others' to fulfill you, all come from the 'amnesia' fogging your mind, from the moment you are born, till the moment you are 're born'.

This book is not a feel good spiritual publication designed to make you feel better about yourself, '*you*' don't exist.

Together, with this book as an aid in learning about your true Self, we will collaborate to begin to get cozy with the principles of spiritual life that will someday bring you answer to the greatest question of all mankind.

"What AM I?"

No matter what 'level' of learning you're at in life, remember this, "I am always learning about MYSELF"

What you see around you is nothing but the witness to your body, eyes, ears, thinking, touching everything… it's all you can know, at least that's what your 'ego' wants you to think!

EGO is your enemy; you cannot fight it, which only verifies it. It actually does not exist … it is the voice in your head that tells you what to do, what to wear, eat, say, think etc…

It is a pre 'programmed' system, a kind of a guide if you like… it is designed to help you find your way through the physical realm as you journey on the travels of your Soul!

Ego is also designed to 'KEEP YOU HERE', lifetime after lifetime…. Through teaching you to JUDGE everything around you into dualistic categories (good bad, right wrong, better worse, black white, etc.) it gets you buying into the world to a fully engaged state, so that you actually believe you are that body and that like everything else around you, you will someday die!

But this is not true!

Together, we will begin to re program/realign the ego compartment of your MIND; transform your thinking, to give you a new way to begin to see things, a new way to look at the world and your place within it; a new point of FOCUS for your mind.

Together, we will break the cycle of rebirth in the 3rd dimension, and the experiences you have that show you my words are true will cement in place a new foundation for living, in you!

A LIFE UNUSUAL

How is it that a life should be?

There is no handbook at birth and from birth to death, life's subtle emotional intricacies and obvious gross contrasts and inequalities certainly don't leave any doubt that only a genius could maneuver its minefield of constant adjustments unscathed.

I have not come through it unscathed, but I have been liberated from the minefield of chaos I once called my life. How exactly it happened can truly only be called a miracle, and definitely by Gods' grace…

I will attempt to tell my story as best I can, but given my increase of diminishing memory and drive for temporal existence this may yet again turn out to be another of my half-finished productions. There are many!

So why write? What for… to leave a document in witness of an event widely unheard of, to those I leave behind in my passing? Perhaps to try and locate myself, my passage through time and space…like a man adrift on a raft might desperately strain his eyes looking for distant landforms…I write because it is Gods' will, simple.

 Gods' will (being love) belies the admonition that all that matters is Love… if this document leads anyone, beggar or king to that realization in their own consciousness, then all efforts to overcome that I have employed and struggled through in my own life will not have been for nothing.

I have had many students of spiritual aspiration through the years. Some who have lived with me in extended collaborative training periods and many who come and go, seemingly deaf and blind to what I espouse and represent.

At the time of this writing, I have no students, my wife and I are busily endeavoring to complete details in readiness for our new healing center (Avatar) opening, the children are in bed asleep and the house is quiet.

I have precious little time for luxuries such as writing from the heart and in my heart tonight I truly hope that my words will reflect mercy and make some kind of sense.

There is a great urgency to this work and a sense that I must make it as available as possible, as quickly as possible…it's difficult to explain this, but if I say 'I have an assignment to fulfill' I expect some of you will get it.

I am completely accustomed to being misunderstood of course, even the historic Jesus said "only 2 in 10 000 will hear this", and from my own interactions with people from all walks, I have encountered no evidence to the contrary to prove Jesus' words inaccurate.

But try I must, an unusual life such as mine, recognized by me as being rare indeed in recorded human accomplishment, must be documented, for the greater good of humanity as a whole and for the good of you, the reader now!

Be thorough in your reading of these pages, you are not reading a tabloid or a fictional work. You may at times think I am completely mad, but remember… you have absolutely nothing to lose, we are One and your time is counting down as is mine! This book is a journal of sorts. My notes and memories (mostly post enlightenment) that for whatever reason have survived with me these past 19 years, to make it to your attention now.

Am I mad, oh yes, but a mad man who knows as such is in fact sane.

It is the well-adjusted man, the man who thinks that the entire world is crazy and he himself the only clear head in it, who is the danger to himself and all others.
Him who seeks for power(s), him who wants and needs, strives and connives to bring his lot into alignment as he sees fit.
These kinds of men populate the world, are meant to... for this is the world of Death, where all things come to die and experience duality, that good and bad of life that can pick us up on high, or crash us down to the depths of despair.

WELCOME TO THE WORLD

As you read through these pages, your own life will become apparent to you, that which you label 'you' will hopefully stand in stark contrast to principles and paradigms herein detailed.

ANECDOTES

1994

1994. Whilst working as a gardener on Long Isle, Whitsundays, beset with alcohol addiction, completely frustrated with all my meditative efforts to date, I met a man called Richard, the island garbo.

Richard and I had been having some biblical chats, we often sat in the work shed after the other lads had gone home and he would tell/guide me in matters about God and his faith.

The other guys all thought him weird, as he didn't drink... In Queensland where I live, EVERYONE who works a blue-collar job drinks.

Upon him resigning/leaving the island, he gave me a copy of the good news bible, suggesting I read the book of Jeremiah, which I did.

Immediately I had renewed vigor for meditation and inquiry. I grew my hair and decided that on my next day off I would venture deep into the bush to establish a private place to meditate that was quiet, away from the resort, staff quarters etc.

On the day I took a bag with incense, some food and water, and began along the 'circuit track', a 3-4 km national parks track that had several beautiful scenic tourist viewing areas and a few interesting old trees to see.

As I began out along the track, I had walked no more than 100 meters when I began to 'vibrate', every cell in my body felt 'activated'.
All of a sudden it felt as if two hands gripped me beneath my armpits and I became feather light, as if I had no weight at all, my feet were now physically barely on the ground... I heard a soft voice in my head, not male or female, "Don't be afraid".

'Feather light' may be apt as I do recall having the distinct feeling I was in the company of angels.... though to this day I still have no confirmed opinion whether I believe in angels.

I don't recall now what I was thinking at that moment, but I was 'carried' at speed up the track, past the banyan tree and off into the untracked bush, up and up the mountain side to almost the top, and then I was at a small clearing and everything stopped.

As I looked about I noticed many stones in the vicinity and was suddenly overcome with the strong desire to build a stone circle.

I knew there would be 21 stones somehow, and I counted them when I had finished, and there was. (a year later on the moors in Plymouth England, I encountered a larger stone circle, also having 21 stones)

I sat on the altar stone in the center and decided this was a great place to meditate, but for some reason, on that day I didn't.

I did however say a prayer, burn the incense and sat long and long wondering about my life and what had just happened.

As with all my 'experiences' associated with the spiritual realm I recall feeling unexcited somewhat and looking back it seemed that I ought to have been more concerned/interested in the experience(s) itself that day. It is odd, I find that I am so 'easy going' with it...

As for the stone circle, it's still there, overgrown, the bush land reclaiming the clearing.
Several years ago I revisited the spot, and re cleared it a bit, considering it as somehow a kind of sacred spot.

I don't know any more than that really, but I did meet a woman in Canberra some years later who told me that I opened a 'lay line', though I never really investigated that idea or have any clue about lay lines.

Peace

AMACHI

Amachi (The Mother)

Much is said about the mother, but this is my tale.

For those who haven't heard of her, Amachi is a realized woman from India, of whom it is said, miracles follow her wherever she goes.

I once saw a video of her turn water into milk pudding in front of a crowd, who then proceeded to hail her and cast flowers at her feet and head. There are endless charlatans and conjurers in India posing as holy men and for a while I considered her no more clever nor authentic than these. But time and witness were to prove me wrong.

Amachi travels the world, seeking out wealthy western patrons to fund her many orphanages and schools in India. She is often known to travel with these patrons and take accommodations with them.

The time I went to see the mother was one of these times. She was travelling Australia with her entourage and was coming to the Gold Coast not more than two hours from where we all were in NSW at the spiritual centre I was living/studying at.

My teacher gave a short talk about her the day before and asked if anyone was keen to go see "a genuine guru".

There were a few at the center who had already had several contacts with Amachi and on this occasion it was known that two of our 'ex' center attendees were funding this leg of the mothers tour and would be with her on the podium the next night in the honored position of attendants/helpers.

. A lovely 'spiritual' couple who for reasons of eastern association were disenchanted with my loudmouth American teacher and had decided to leave the center to seek gentler spiritual vernacular.

Needless to say there was a certain amount of consternation regarding them and the general situation with the center at the time as one of them it seemed had vested financial interests in the center's running at earlier days and was seemingly unimpressed with the 'authenticity' or authority of my teacher, whom I knew to be authentic by my own divine revelations.

It's a case of the old saying "don't judge a book by its cover."

I thought of the situation, "What did it matter your guide through hell, so long as you were willing to do as they directed?" Who cared if they chanted or if they bellowed…it's Hell.

So the next evening about seven or eight of us drove up to the venue to see Amachi. There were about a thousand people crammed into the basketball hall/auditorium with a big eastern style podium, musicians and food vendors… quite a put on! Eventually she came out and read something from the Gitas in Hindi (I think), and in an English translation.

Then there were the hugs.

Amachi is renowned for her deep motherly hugs. As there were so many in the hall, they were handing out tickets for the hugs, so I decided not to bother. But the 'energy' was so high in the hall I couldn't sit on the floor like all the devotees, so instead I went up beside the podium and 'released' my light. I was so 'high' on the energy there that I couldn't contain myself, hopping about and moving like a crazy man beside the stage.

(To the uninitiated it would have looked like I was doing some kind of weird dance). I recall the mother having a twinkle in her eye as we caught eye contact a moment… a nice moment.

Then the hugs started, and as I watched, I suddenly spotted the two ex's right beside her on the podium, being ushered into special place by her regular helpers/handmaidens.

I scanned the long cue of devotees and found my teacher, his partner and I think two other of our group a fair way back in the line. They didn't come all this way not to get one of her legendary hugs I guess.

I waited and danced all the while till they got closer, then I went round to the front to observe the show. I noticed that the two ex-attendees also had spotted my teacher and brethren in the line and were, to me, seemingly somewhat disarmed at the fact.

So as the cue got shorter, each person hugs the mother, she utters 'Amma Amma Amma' in their ears and gives them a small chocolate, then leaves the stage, ushered off by helpful hands. (*It is customary in India for the guru to give the student a gift, for it is the student who gives the spiritual gift of self-awareness/union to the guru.*)

Then it was my teachers' partners turn. She went up the few steps of the podium, knelt and hugged, received the chocolate and exit stage left… Then my teacher approached. Ignoring the two white clothed sponsors on his immediate right, he hugged the mother and she held him.

Everyone else's hug was a matter of one… two…seconds, but this hug, seemed a good five or six seconds. And as the mother gestured to her aide to bring his partner back onto the podium and as the three of them group hugged for another ten seconds. I noticed the two ex's beside watching on, turning to look at each other in seeming dismay.

Here was their new guru, validating (wordlessly) my guru, the same man they had denied some months earlier.

The ideas I had about charlatanism and conjuring of the mother's authenticity vanished. There was no way she could have known who my teacher was. I was both pleased I went to see her and pleased that the tense situation I was privy to between all involved seemed resolved. The both of them at certain times returning in friendship to the center on the odd occasion.

COBBER AND LAURIE

The following section is comprised from accounts of the more prominent lessons I encountered with my early days in mind training. They center on defenselessness and give - the two main actions of mind in Christ consciousness.

Cobber and Laurie:

Cobber was my dog. A smallish very intelligent cattle cross kelpie. Laurie was a brother at the Center, an old, ex alcoholic, ready for the great beyond, very beautiful person inside, very bad breath.

For a few years, Cobber and I lived in my van in the garage out back of the center. I had the duty to be a kind of night watchmen, checking the gates and center doors were locked for the night after ten pm. There were half a dozen cabins on the center grounds too with a few brothers in each, all live in residents, permanent students/teachers of the Course.

It wasn't a bad place to hang out. Always someone to talk to and during peak light integration times, whilst enduring the seeming endless bouts of sleepless nights, I could always find a light on and a bro to have a hot chocolate with.

Every now and then, being so close to the heart of Byron Bay town, a reflection of some messianic idea or another would wander in and attempt to sermonize us with ranting unintelligible, babble stemming forth from a past experience of some light connection not properly integrated. Nut houses are full of people who have seen God and believe they are Jesus or Buddha or someone high ranking.

I saw that in myself early on, thinking/wondering if I too was the reincarnation of a prophet etc. Thankfully I had the course and many grounded brothers about me during that time of mind upheaval.

Anyhow, there was a rule around the center - NO DOGS.

I seemed to get around it since Cobber and I were there before the rule was introduced.
However, whilst rules were only in place mainly so as to check box an individual's resistance to authority, they were mostly never enforced unless the rule concerned dealt with the common welfare of all or individual safety/consciousness. E.g. No Drugs.

There were sticklers for rules however and Laurie was one of those brothers. He was an old 12 step AA guy. A very powerful, uncompromising mind when he wanted to be and he didn't take well to me or my dog. I always considered it an old school new school thing and try as I might; it took many years of self-confrontation and acceptance before I finally felt peace in my relationship with him.

I was conscious that I held him as a kind of mentor, but also saw that I did not really relate much to him. I had dropped the identity of alcoholic through grace, in one swoop, but he had struggled with it over most of his whole life.

I think he resented me for that for some reason. In the early days/months of my time at Byron, he would mutter one word at me every time we passed by each other ... 'asshole'.

The confusion I/we held regarding our relationship for each other as Christ brothers bobbed in and out of awareness over several years. I always thought we should just be happy, but personally, I never got that reflection back from him or rarely anyway.

Things eventually came to a head between us with my dog Cobber as the catalyst. After session each day, we could have a lunch break and usually, during summer months, most brothers would go to eat under the shade of the big fig tree in the courtyard out back.

There was a skinny ramp leading from the back of the indoor dining room out to the tree and there was a small grassed area beside the courtyard too, where some brothers would eat occasionally and where I sometimes tied Cobber whilst I was in a session.

I had had Cobber since a pup. I got him from the pound, the last remaining pup, the runt of a litter that had all died from parvo. Initially, Cobber used to wail and bark when I was in session but he soon grew accustomed to his place out back. He was a good guard dog, several times alerting me to intruders after dark, in which one time eventuated in a necessity to call the police.

But Laurie didn't like Cobber. The rules said he shouldn't be allowed, and that was that. At lunch times, I often had verbal altercations with Laurie about Cobber. I never liked these occasions. Laurie went on and on.
He had a dead man's breath, a legacy of his liver degradation and green corpse like skin. Alcoholism is a terrible addiction,

just as bad on family and friends as the addict.

But I knew Laurie was an opportunity for forgiveness, to heal a relationship and to integrate that within myself as I continued to true up to Christ mindedness. I knew there was no Laurie and no Cobber but here was a situation playing itself out in form, so I decided to use/heal it in form.

Day after day passed by over about a six month period, during which time I must have had at least seven or eight shouting matches with Laurie about Cobber. "Dogs have worms, kids get worms from dogs, dogs poo on grass" etc.

As each encounter happened, resolve in me grew, determination to face the next encounter/barrage with the principles of the Course. I studied and studied, I sought advice from other brothers, some sympathetic to Laurie. Eventually it sprung out at me . . . DEFENSELESSNESS.

The next time I encountered Laurie, I would stand defenselessly, honestly letting in whatever Laurie/my mind was attempting to tell me. It is an energetic thing, a frequency of healing if seen correctly.

The words are nothing in themselves, simply carriers of encoded information utilizable in unlocking inner doorways, based on the initial calling to God for healing and peace of mind.

So it was Wednesday afternoon, I was eating my lunch under the tree, there would have been about fifty brothers there too, enjoying the sun and outdoors lunch together. Laurie wasn't out there. I had a small foreboding feeling every time I couldn't see him; he was like a character from the Munsters, lurching about somewhere.

By this time I was dreading the confrontation I knew was

looming with Laurie. I really just wanted to tell him to fuck off and stop being such a 'wally' but I knew that wasn't the solution. I needed this lesson learned in me or I knew it would present again in yet another form, dragging out space and time in my own association unnecessarily.

I looked at my empty plate and started thinking about hitting the beach for a swim. I saw myself walking across the courtyard, up the ramp, plate in the kitchen and I was free. I could almost feel the water and the terrifying anticipation of confrontation.

I stood up in dread, no Laurie in sight. I crossed the courtyard and started up the skinny ramp.

Laurie.

Half way up, he was half way down, his plate full, mine empty, a standoff.
Right away the barrage started, dog this, dog that, on and on for what seemed like an age. Inside I wanted to burst, there was so much I could say, so many reasonably spiritual points of view…but I knew they were all bullshit now.

The one thing I had chosen to stay true to was defenselessness. I would not utter a word, and more than that, I would try to honestly listen and let in what he was saying, despite my own inner rebellion telling me not to. It was hard. I genuinely wanted to get through this and I also really wanted to lash out…I saw my inner conflict….Be still I told myself, this can't last forever.

A few brothers had backed up behind me on the skinny ramp, unable to get past; enjoying the show I'll bet. It was always a laugh to watch the showdowns of other brothers transformational processes, but it wasn't ever fun being at high noon yourself.

After what seemed a long time, Laurie fell quiet. Was that it? Could we now edge past each other on that ramp and carry on our respective days? "Are you done?" I asked him, not wanting to sound smarmy. He said nothing, pushing past me down the ramp to eat his lunch.

I spent the day at the beach, feeling uncertain about the situation and its resolution.

Next morning I was on kitchen roster, doing prep for lunch, Laurie was in charge of the kitchen for that day. Feelings of apprehension flooded me as I sheepishly said good morning to him, but to my surprise, he turned and smiled at me, gave me a big hug, uttering only....thank you.

From then on, things between us were great, not better, great…the principle of defenselessness was now my greatest ally, one I would call upon in many times to come.

CONFRONTING THE BOYS

This story relates to two separate incidents that happened to me requiring my faith during the times I spent teaching at Tilba Tilba.

Several times each week, about a dozen of us would gather at Sue's house on the lake to do 'light sessions' and study from 'A Course in Miracles'. John was a huge gentle man who towered over me several inches who I recall had hands as big as dinner plates.

From the outset as a mind awakened, I was aware that ALL participants are not there as they claim, to seek the light, for if that were true, they would have found it already, being as there is absolutely no block to an unequivocal appeal for truth.

Reaching this point however is in the main, what removing the blocks to loves awareness through 'A Course In Miracles' is all about.

As a 'teacher/guide' through this mental minefield of transformation, I took it upon myself that regardless of the singular nature of my own association, I am in service to whomever turns up for this purpose and should therefore assume that whomever does show up for one of my sessions is under the awareness that I will avail to them of absolutely any input I am given as internal guidance for them, regardless of how it may make them feel, react etc.

I learned early on that refusing to impart what is channeled through Christ for a brother only leads to further chaos and lack of peace.

This often became personally confronting, (the mutual nature of healing), as Christ consciousness has no limits, no political correctness, no concern for reciprocity or good relations and no concern for the welfare of the messenger, me.

In general, despite my apprehensions at times, things in this regard always worked out extremely well and I had learned to trust my inner guidance no matter what personal standpoints of limitation it brought up within me.

So back at Tilba, over the months, I realized that John was not there at each session solely to pursue the removal of whatever blocks he may have had, but was it seemed to me, more interested in pursuing a deeper relationship with Sue, which unless he became 'fully' aware of, would cloud his ability to continue releasing all dependencies/attachments of temporal associations.

I knew that at the point of realization of his private agenda situation that he would have to make a decision. On the one hand salvation makes no compromise and his transformation would not be ongoing and continue to unfold unless he relinquished all specialness he was projecting subconsciously onto Sue. And on the other he would have to recognize that his efforts at salvations means were on false foundations.

This of course is no different to many confrontations with falsity I myself had made (*and continue to make*) over the years and I scoured my mind deeply for a few days to try to reveal my own falsity in this situation, as I did not wish to negate the fact that all my observations are merely my mirror.

Not finding any loss of peace personally I decided to turn my thinking on the matter over to the Holy Spirit and leave any further dealings on the subject in higher hands than mine.

It was only a few days until our next 'light session' and it was then that my inner guidance spilled out and over the cup of my consciousness and took form as a flurry of powerful/confrontational words directed squarely at John.

As I recall thinking at the time, 'Oh lord, here we go' and wondering whether he might throw me out a window or something. But I took stock in the Lord and simply said what I had to say in as gentle and considerate a way as came to me, which, if you knew me then, was a miracle in itself.

As I began addressing him, amidst the gathering of his friends and peers, John stood up to face me in the center of the room, and stood silent. I continued on calmly explaining the situation as it appeared to me, and the silence of all gathered became deafening.

But to my surprise, when I finished my tirade, John just stood silently, and then with the innocence of a child who had just learned the facts about Santa, he turned to Sue and asked if she felt what I had said was accurate. As she answered in angelic honesty, he started to cry a little, turned back to me and hugged me firmly.

There was a very great release in that big man in that moment, a big unrealized burden now revealed, was dropped. John was now standing in the center of his rebirth, his choice for Truth before him clearly.

It was not long after that day that I again packed and left to return to Nth NSW.
John didn't turn up at sessions for a while and before long the crew there disbanded as often happens in this pursuit, and the small healing portal, its use fulfilled, closed its doors.

I did hear that John had gone on to develop some sort of a forgiveness program for children and that every one of whom I asked about his wellbeing said he was happy and grateful for his life now.

And I saw my fears for my physical security clearly exposed - a David and goliath moment for me!

Afterwards, I realized the moment of releasing my own fears in the lead up to that day, the failure I had to live in love as I taught, the disappointment I had in my own self worth seeing the doubt and fear I had in a relationship I had supposedly given to God.

I recall that I thought it strange I couldn't detect my insincerity prior but I now never underestimate the cunning and baffling nature of ego.

PAUL

Paul was a Course teacher from America, who, with his partner had decided to stay a while in Tilba and sit in on our sessions.

Everyone was very happy about having a 'brother' who had sat with the 'Master Teacher' in Wisconsin, and I myself was pleased to have someone whom was capable of 'holding' a light session.

The crew at Tilba, by this stage, was quite steady on their feet with the basis of the 'Course' thought system and I had been encouraging them to take turns 'hosting' a session here and there as they felt guided to do. Sue was especially capable and often liked to lead the group in my absence.

After a month or so, it was brought to my attention, that during my absences from sessions that Paul was interruptive and was correcting the hosts of each session, something that is definitely not the go in 'course' curriculum.

As this situation was brought to my attention, I supposed I had better include it into my own consciousness as a reflection of my own denial of perfection and see where that led me.

One of the basic principles of spirituality is that there's no one to heal except yourself - no one else to correct. All form is illusory, so to buy into the drama of one person's efforts/life even in a spiritually evolving sense is simply to buy into error.

I sat a while, considering the notifications I had received about Paul and asking within for guidance in dealing with the situation externally should it need be.

Well a few days passed and it was my turn to host a session… Paul and his wife were present.
At about half way in, I decided that as an attempt to clarify various concepts regarding conscious/sub conscious levels of mind that I would draw diagrams on the white board. I knew that what I was drawing and how I was explaining things was being well received by the crew but I sensed Paul's mind was like a coiled spring.

From my understanding of the training received at the center in Wisconsin I knew that rarely did students hold sessions and almost never did a white board get used to express conceptual ideas such as I was now doing. And, from my memory of things at the time I recall thinking that Paul was someone held in quite high regard as a 'light/bright' Brother.

I recall my teacher's eyeballs often shooting skyward at various snippets of 'Master Teacher/Academy news', and it was understood amongst most of the crew I knew from Byron Bay, that the colloquialisms "Master Teacher, Bright One and Dear One" had become statements much like backhanded compliments.

There were many individuals from the 'Academy' who in my view had been there so long that they had become institutionalized and had become stagnated in their transition process. This happens in all institutional settings from universities to rehab centers.

There are always those to whom the actual life cloistered away from the dramas of external life is preferable to that they assume awaits them outside.

This of course is neither good nor bad, as from a singular perspective I am only ever being shown my own path even if it is through recognition of another's.

I recognized early on that even the idea of a healing center was something to transit through, to be left behind when its usefulness was done. And that even the vernacular and conceptual association fostered by the center was a limit on learning.

I saw the center as a stepping stone to what lay beyond as part and parcel of learning how to recognize constantly what was always right in front of my face…Christ.

Recognizing Paul's obvious irritation at my presentation, I made a hurried internal appeal to Spirit to help me should there be an outburst, at which exact point there was.

Paul shot up and said in an obviously excited voice, "I just have to say…" At which point I spontaneously returned fire with, "NO, you don't just have to say anything!"

He fell silent as I continued; words flowing through me like the biblical Jesus addressing the temple sellers directly…passionate and powerful.

"There is nothing you need to say to me, nor to any of these," as I gestured with my hand at the other students seated about the room, "You are here to include in whatever shows up for you just as these students are…"

I seemed to deliberately include him into the rank of student rather than to acknowledge any 'Teacher' status he may have assumed as a "Bright One" from the U.S.

I continued on a bit and concluded with, "You are welcome to sit and 'listen' or leave." At which he left, leaving his red faced wife sitting amongst us all, who after a moment's consideration also left.

I recall feeling a little shaken after that confrontation, but the principle was sound upon which I stood and I realized that the admonition, "Only an awakened mind can teach this course" was suddenly blazoned across the threshold of my consciousness, like some kind of confirmation.

I felt that somehow I had completed some kind of exam, some rite of passage.

I laughed at the notion out loud later that day as I sat and contemplated over and over how things might have been if I had reacted differently.

I recall thinking that I had 'accepted' myself at a higher level of service somehow, and then laughed aloud at that too. It was a weird afternoon for me, taking on my own ideas of 'Master teachers' and so on...

I realized that I was free from that nonsense now too, and that the admonition "Call No Man Master" was now fluent and active within me.

Paul returned to the house several days later whilst we were all gathered in the big country kitchen over hot drinks. As he entered the room he was warmly greeted. He came directly over to me and bent down to give me a big hug. I realized he too had had a shift and I embraced him in the joy of our mutual progress.

It was a big day for Love!

MY ENLIGHTENMENT

Introduction:

There are many concepts that are bandied round in spiritual circles as to what awakening and enlightenment is. The following document is strictly regarding enlightenment and the non-temporal experience that it is gained through.

This is not an out of body experience. This is an experience of no body, no world, no universe whatsoever. As described in Hindu texts it is an experience of direct emersion and dissolvement into the Godhead.

Awakening, through my own experiences and understandings is merely the process of remembering (*whether enlightened or not*); where you are and what you are always.

At some point in your life whether in this lifetime or another, you will experience your own enlightenment simply because the time and place it is destined to happen is set within you already. Once it is experienced it can never be denied.

In A Course In Miracles, Jesus states, "this is so rare on earth, that if it happens, so be it, if it does not happen, so be it as well'.

Time does not flow in a sequential manner. It exists as one moment always which is commonly termed as 'the now'. This will only make full sense to the human mind through the actual experience of enlightenment.

I do not intend to start a conceptual ping pong match with those of you who already learned religious/spiritual doctrines and concepts. I am merely trying to express the inexpressible the best I can based on my limited understanding of the general theme of spirituality.

To this day I live 24/7 with the recognition of two realities in my mind; the eternal and the physical.

In my early years I made futile attempts to correlate these two understandings as I tried to maintain some grip of my sanity, post experience.

I learned through great angst and head banging conceptual walls that the two cannot be synchronized as a single consciousness, as a single point of view without much ordeal or purification.

The following document was originally written less than 12months after my enlightenment as an attempt to keep its integrity and virtue intact as a first hand reference, it has been little changed up until this printing.

TESTIMONIAL

This is the story of my awakening, a truly biblical style happening which saw me hurled from the physical realm into the formlessness of God, to remember everything that is and return to earth with that knowledge for the greater good of all mankind.

Staying true to that experience has been a real roller coaster ride, which is only now, seven years later, beginning to level out and let me truly rest in the peace of the revelation that day's happening showed me.

One month prior to my thirty third birthday, at the edge of a Stanley knife I surrendered to God, in a gut wrenching appeal for forgiveness, understanding, help and purpose. God answered me in four words, spoken from within my own mind and resounding throughout the outer universe, just like a Cecil B Demille movie. I followed the direction of those four words . . . .

But this document would lack relativity/dimension, if I failed to outline the circumstances of my life prior to this, perhaps your story is or was a little like mine, perhaps nothing like it.

From my earliest self-aware moments I knew I was different from almost all the other kids at my school. I realized that there was something fundamentally wrong with the ways of the world and although I couldn't put a finger on it I felt that there was something missing or something I was here to do. I felt the meaningless of the world and wondered what I was here for . . .

To me, looking back, I had a weird and almost surreal childhood. And despite the awkwardness of puberty and its emotional tug of war, I couldn't wait to find what was next for me. It seems to me that looking back, I was always looking ahead, never content, a dreamer…

I started smoking pot at the age of fourteen, which changed my outlook on life totally. Whilst initially only for teenage fun, it soon became a means of escape from the meaninglessness of what I called my life and I began to make decisions regarding my entire life revolving around my ability to stay stoned. I theorized that if I felt good like this all the time, I wouldn't care what I was doing for a job, or worry about anything at all actually.
But I did not realize that I was comfortably numb!

After leaving home in my late teens/twenties I travelled to the outback and to the Whitsundays where I learned to drink, heavily. At least four and five nights each week saw me pass out about three or four am, staggering in from bars and clubs, (*often alone, but occasionally with some random female attached*), only to go to work, gardening, with a massive hangover.

A failed engagement and subsequent suicide attempt (call for help) saw me wake up in Mackay base hospital, which truly only marked the beginning of the next ten years of alcoholism, drug abuse and more failed relationships. Lies and deceit saw me back flipping and hiding from almost all my friends at one time or another.

After a million utterances of "*I'm never drinking again*" I would eventually leave the Whitsundays and move to a house, which my beautifully supportive parents brought for me, in the country. My parents I guess I would describe as open minded and accepting of my ism's, I think they had great concerns at that time, but they were happy just to know I was happy, and so I did not drag them into my malaise quest any more than I had to.

Drinking this whole time I practiced a form of meditation I taught myself after a few visits to a hypnotist *(for a flaccidity-alcohol/drug related problem)* which I merged with an open eye practice I learned from the Brahma Kamari

Whilst practicing this inner journeying I had several occurrences of stigmata/bleeding, from the birthmark in the center of my forehead and experienced a kind of faint light which seemed shielded by a grey veil of some sort.

Whilst practicing this meditation one night, on the back beach of one of the Whitsunday Islands, I was interrupted by a couple of lovers. As I was naked, *(trying to get closer to God)*, I decided to go on my next day off from work there, as a gardener, into the national park, to look for a private meditation spot where I would be in solitude.

On the day, I took a bible which Richard the garbo had given me, some incense, grapes, a candle and a bottle of water. As I headed off on the circuit track walk, I was very peaceful and happy to be putting so much effort into my spiritual side of life and away from parties and girls and alcohol.

After I had walked about one hundred meters I noticed a vibrating sensation throughout my body, which grew to a pronounced intensity within seconds, so much so I became worried and tried to turn back.

It was when I realized that I couldn't turn around that I became really worried, my feet seemed cemented to the track. Then I heard a voice in my mind, which said, "Don't be afraid." Suddenly my fear went and I became feather light, my feet seemed to be barely on the ground and I realized I was being sort of carried.

I could still feel my feet moving, but there was a sensation of hands under my armpits, lifting me and guiding me along. I was moving at a rapid pace, faster than mere walking or jogging, like fast-forward on a video movie.

I was carried up the track, and past the end of the track and into the untracked tropical bush island.

Up a mountain ridge I went, almost to the top, then it stopped, the hands, the vibration, being carried . . . nothing. I was suddenly overcome with the impulse to build a stone circle there in that place, and I set about it with fervor. I didn't count the stones, but I knew there would be 21, and there was.

After rolling a large flat altar stone into the middle, I sat on it and read my bible, lit the candle and incense and said some prayers. I also discovered a small stone spire built from small round rocks near that place. I figured it for either an aboriginal grave or a treasure site. Cannon balls had been found on the island.

Nothing else happened that day and I went home late in the afternoon feeling strangely, a little flat. There was no one I knew to whom I could tell of this day though this experience was the first major turning point in my faith, which showed me that there was something else, perhaps angels.

Many years later I would meet a woman in Canberra, now a close friend, who told me of a little book she had once read about ley lines, and of the stories like mine, of others who had also built circles, inspired in a similar way.

All these experiences saw me become more withdrawn from my external world and despite the obvious clash with my hopeless state of external affairs; I began to raise the ideas to mind that I was on a spiritual journey and paid attention to those ideas more and more.

I left that place and travelled a bit, and through the fog of alcohol and drugs, ideas and people of a spiritual nature began to eventuate in my life more and more frequently.

After travelling Europe and eventually returning to Australia to once again work in the Whitsundays, I again fell into drug and alcohol abuse to try and stave off the meaninglessness of my life.

I had a few profound satanic experiences on LSD and decided that was not for me. I was also battling an enormous guilt complex over a termination I forced my girlfriend at the time to have, something which would eventually be a major catalyst in bringing me to my dark night of the soul.

I decided to leave the area and move south, away from the thirty one clubs and bars of the tiny Airlie Beach strip. I remember thinking that when I had moved to that area many years ago there were only two places in town you could get a drink, never a truer representation of my own inner situation.

My parents and I spent a few months scouring the hills and dales of Northern New South Wales, renowned for its freaks, hippies, rednecks and alternatives. We eventually found a house on Bald Mountain, and it would be here I would have my Jesus experience.

Here in the lush green hippy hills I met odd and diverse thinking folks like myself, spirituals, religious, Hare Krishna's, Buddhists, Osho Sannyasins and environmentalists . . . I reveled in it all. I had cut drinking down to a six-pack a day, increased my pot smoking, growing a few nice plants to keep me honest and was enjoying gardening.

I embraced the primary beliefs of many religions and continued to have a few profound path confirming experiences Meeting Jesus one morning after spending a lonely night atop Mt Warning after asking him for spiritual guidance the night before in prayer was one of them..

On the first day I stood on the land of my new block looking at Mt Warning, I experienced a sensation of my feet being glued to the spot. Magnetized is actually more like it. I was struck dumb at what was happening and all I could do was stare straight ahead at Mt Warning.

I recall feeling like I was vulnerable, I could hear my parents talking to the realtor inside the house and I hoped they would not call me in, I felt as if no one should know I was glued to the spot.

And just then I had a thought to go spend a night on the summit. Someone had told me that on full moon nights there were gatherings of folks up there celebrating whatever, some pagan thing or another, but I knew somehow that I didn't want to do it for any reason I could as yet discern.

My feet became free, life went on. I set about building vegetable gardens, looking for work (which I never found) and planting some dope.

Years before when I was still in the Whitsundays, I met a Native American chap, Joey (now gone to the happy hunting ground). He and I had gotten drunk one night whilst talking all manner of spiritual stuff and had smashed a glass and cut each other's palms and become blood brothers.

I don't know if that was disrespectful of any true custom but we were true in spirit so we didn't really care. I later took him to my stone circle where we held a small formal ceremony to mark our bond. He strung an eagle feather I had given him from tree branches about the circle and had sung a song in his native tongue (Navajo).

Because of that meeting, Native American philosophies had become strong in me and I had come into possession of a few peyote cactus which when dried into buttons were eaten by native Americans to induce shaman visions. I decided to take some peyote to Mt Warning and try it there one night soon.

On the afternoon I finally went up the mountain, I took several leather medicine bags which I made and sometimes sold at local markets, a mars bar, a candle and some matches. I forgot my peyote, something which depressed me a little when I discovered it was missing, upon reaching the summit.

As night began to fall it started raining, a steady drizzle which soaked me through. It was bitterly cold. My buckskin jacket, warm as it usually was, gave no defense against the rain. There was no natural cover or man-made shelter up there, only waist high stubby brush and bushes.

I set my candle in the center of the summit, set four medicine bags in each direction hanging from the bushes and I said a prayer. I called upon the spirits of the four directions to blow away the rain, and then I curled up in the open grass and tried to get some sleep, drizzle still falling steadily, teeth chattering.

I was beginning to think that this was a dumb idea, but I had no torch and it was too dark to go back down. I curled up in the long wet grass, rain still drizzling on my face. I shared the mars bar with a large black possum (*my totem*) and fell into a light sleep.

Estimating some fifteen minutes to have passed I was awoken by a howling wind, seeming to blow from all directions. It howled like a hurricane and all the brush swished and bowed, my long hair snapped back and forth. I sat upright, staring into the dark, shivering, hugging my knees. Then it stopped as suddenly as it started, and I was blessed with a still and starry night all night. I didn't sleep well, but I was a little happier to be drying out.

At about what I guessed to be four am, I heard voices coming from the track below me, and within a few minutes I was introducing myself to four people who had come to watch the sun come up. They introduced themselves to me as the spirits of the four directions, North, South, East and West. I was dumbfounded, and I showed them the medicine bags still hanging from the bushes in each direction and the prayer I had offered.

None of us knew how to react to the next moment and we all stood in a kind of laughing disbelief for what seemed an age.

We all settled into a kind of meditative expectancy of the sunrise on the east facing open mesh platform, and waited. Minutes later we were interrupted by four American camera toting tourists, clad in the latest spandex, Nike/Adidas brand sports and mountain climbing apparel. "Oh look honey, people meditating, take a photo, take a photo."

Yes our peace was shattered, but we all ignored them, as if by unspoken agreement, and we resumed our wait. Within myself I asked Jesus for some clear direction for my life.

The sun rose and the tourists had wandered off to the south platform. It was suddenly very quiet.

Then, in the back regions of my mind a voice spoke to me that I had never heard before, but that I recognized, Jesus, "Do whatever you want, just don't let go of my hand."

My life changed from that day, although I didn't understand how to utilize the change and it kind of got lost, but I couldn't forget that voice, ever.

Whilst living at that house in the lush green hills, I had experiences of the devil, insanity, death, and community love and rainbow tribe harmony. I grew my hair into dreadlocks and started wearing nothing but a sarong. I felt really free.

But it did not last. Eventually, after a few years, it too all became just a ritual of trying to fit in to some other identity or someone else's ways of life and that feeling that I didn't belong soon re-emerged and dogged me and saw me return to drinking and drugging again to cope with the collapse of my self-identity and returned meaninglessness of my life.

I had however formed a strong bond with Jesus in my own way and was reading the Sermon on the Mount in the New Testament of the bible almost daily, over and over. This gave me great comfort right up until I realized that the rest of the world obviously hadn't read it.

Forgiveness and love, that was all I wanted, but how to forgive, what to forgive, drove me crazy.

All my life the voice in my head, my thinking me, had been full of shit as well as reasonable stuff, but now the shit was emerging at full throttle, insane thoughts ran naked and exposed through my mind screaming at me to commit suicide, murder, mutilations and mayhem.

My days and night were filled with horrific and depraved images flashing on the screen of my sub consciousness.

I became recluse, afraid to look anyone in the eye. My dreams were vivid and horrible, my awake hours were depressing and mind numbing . . . after almost a year of this non-stop insanity, living from one fantasy escape to another I decided I couldn't take it any longer and would kill myself.

One month prior to my thirty third birthday, at the edge of a Stanley knife I surrendered to God, in a gut wrenching appeal for forgiveness, understanding, help and purpose. God answered me in four words, spoken from within my own mind and resounding throughout the outer universe, just like a Cecil B DE mille movie. I followed the direction of those four words, "Go to Byron Bay."

I had prayed/appealed for inner peace, for some kind of spiritual (non-religious) course to help me and for a way to help others who may be in situations like mine. I felt certain my prayers would be answered.

On the way to Byron Bay I stopped in to collect two friends from a nearby commune, and the three of us had a lovely day in Byron but no divine happening as I was expecting.

For the next three mornings I awoke to Gods voice, again repeating, "Go to Byron Bay." I again collected my spiritual friends and again no happening.

On the last day I heard His voice, I went alone and on entering Byron, I again heard His voice directing me, "Turn left here." I turned left, and not far down that road the car stalled to a stop in front of a small place called the Miracle Centre.

Many, *many*, **many**, incredible stories of healing and miraculous occurrences could be told of the goings on and happenings at this divine portal guised as a healing center, but I will continue with this one for now.

I got out of the car and approached a woman sitting on a small wall outside. I told her about the Voice that had directed me there and asked her what went on here and she told me simply, go inside and listen.

Inside, I realized I was early for whatever was to be the morning service or happening and so I stood and listened to a group of about six people who were reading affirmations aloud at the far end of a large carpeted room.

Not only didn't I understand what they were reading but I also certainly didn't understand why they were laughing so much. I watched a man who had a stroke, one half of his body unresponsive, laugh so hard drool fell from the corner of his open mouth.
I decided that God had sent me to an insane asylum, and considered that it was probably appropriate. I also realized that I

did not know what was happening and that I was judging these people.
 I made a decision not to judge, and then it happened.

In the twinkling of an eye, the people vanished before me and I was staring at a blank wall; the walls of the center then vanished, revealing the outside world, which also then vanished, and then my body vanished.

 I was Light, golden light, mind, in mind, of God mind . . .

God's voice spoke saying, "Nothing Exists."

I was aware of myself as pure thought, I heard me think "What is this?" Which instantly expelled me from that experience and I found myself back in the carpeted room at the other end lying face down on the carpet, surrounded by a circle of about forty smiling people, all holding hands around me, some of them in joyful tears.

The experience of my enlightenment only seemed to last four or five seconds, but back in the room I guess almost twenty minutes had passed. I knew the truth, all of it. I was completely changed, without any ability to go back to my old confused questioning mind.

I got up from my face flat position on the floor, and as I stood up I was looking directly at an old woman and in that instant was washed from head to foot with the most uncontrollable feeling/wave of love. I realized unconditional love right there on earth. I went around the circle of beings there, (40 or so), and hugged them all one by one, with no change in emotion or love from one to the next.

The greatest moment in all time and space anyone could ever experience had just happened to me and I knew it.

I recall thinking that all I wanted was that moment, forever, more than all the worlds' wealth, power or pleasures, more than **anything**.

Amidst the God high I was on and the laughter welling up inside me, I settled down to be taught by a Dutch woman, whom I still consider my mother hen. She told me that I must be very powerful, that she has known people who were seeking that experience for over twenty years, through the Course, still unsuccessful. I recall thinking I had no clue what she was talking about.

In heaven all are equal, but on earth everyone is whatever stage of their journey/transformation, they are at. The Course in Miracles states –*'Equality does not imply homogeneity now.'* She told me so many things, all of which seemed somehow like simpleton's knowledge, but which I realized I never understood prior to that experience.

I initially thought that everyone in that room knew what I now know and was shocked to discover over several years that they all did not. I was befuddled to imagine that there are those still as profoundly asleep/ignorant of love as I was.

To me, after that experience, I was 100% convinced that everyone was simply waiting for me to awaken, and that we would all soon be returning to the light together.

It was a shock when it was explained to me that I had returned to 'time space' before that experience happened, and that I was to learn ACIM to integrate the experience into useful fashion for a Divine purpose. It was a BIG shock.

After returning to my home in the hills a few days later, I resolved to spend all my weekends at the center until my house sold and I could move there to study and eventually teach, full time.

I realized that the experience of God only showed me the truth and that I would have to learn of forgiveness according to Divine interpretation of it and apply it to all my thinking/world to purify my mind and to return or merge with God eternally again in my own awareness.

Through utilizing the training lessons of 'A Course in Miracles', I would train my mind to train itself, although it would be three years of constant hell (self-confrontation) and self-forgiveness before I truly began to see the course working through me as a product of 'Work the program until it works you'.

My main teacher there was uncompromisingly direct with me on many occasions, something I definitely was grateful for (*eventualy*).
I blame him in part, (*thanks to God for him*) for the deep peace of mind that now sees me completely happy and in constant peace.

He was the one who really drummed into me that the true spiritual path had very few flowery trimmings and was mostly a direct journey into my own personal hell to piss on the thimble full of flames, which to me seemed so huge and terrifying.
So when things got uncomfortable and I felt like running (*from my mind*) I knew everything was actually right on track and I was in store for a miracle.

Despite that there were many times I did not understand his ways or teachings, I knew that because I had been sent here by God, and that he was the permanent formal teacher, I would trust him beyond any fear or concern that arose in me, and this trust in him and God served me well and lead me through my own hell and its undoing and set me free. The greatest fear any mind has is to love itself unconditionally.

I never drank again from that day on, and twelve months later I gave up drugs too, all cold turkey through the grace of God. I attended some twelve step meetings to help me stay true and to help me better be of help, and I sat with my teacher (*who was teaching abroad at the time of my awakening*) every day for six years, studying 'A Course in Miracles.'

Many profound spiritual experiences continued happening to and through me for the next six years, and still happen today as I endeavor to continue to stay true to God, as one of his teachers on earth.

The center is now many years closed, having fulfilled its function, and those minds it taught are now infiltrating society across Australia and the world spreading the vibration of love through forgiveness everywhere.

The Course in Miracles is a journey **INTO** fear, to discover your **SELF/GOD**. Do not be surprised when a journey to love confronts you with your blocks/fears to love. Unconditional love/God, is not what you think it is . . . it is beyond human comprehension entirely.

God bless us all . . . everyone.

GIRL IN THE DUNES

After session one morning I decided to walk the twenty minutes into town along the beach. The beach was right in front of the healing center and a favorite place for all the brothers to chill especially after a session.

This day however, there were few people on the beach and this was somewhat surprising as it was a beautiful warm day and the surf was just right for a swim. That beach is by far one of Australia's most beautiful beaches and apart from the main area in front of the town headland car park, seldom busy.

The beach would be approximately 6 km long and ran all the way from the tea tree lakes at one end, to The Pass, a popular surfing spot, at the other, with the town in the middle roughly.

There were often vagrants and perverts in the dunes further down towards the nudie beach (tea tree) end, opposite from the direction I was headed, and I generally avoided going there.

The feeling you get when you finish a 'light' session is clarity, a heightened sense of 'subtle energies' and a kind of deeper feeling of connectedness on the physical plane.

There are many amazing stories of paranormal and metaphysical happenings associated with our light sessions I could go on about, but in the main the purpose of clearing away the dross of your human conceptual consciousness baggage is to be able to access/hear the Holy Spirit more clearly.

On this day, as I walked towards town, I did exactly that.

As I set out on the short walk, ocean to my left, high dunes on my right, I had a sense of 'emptying', as if my insides were being drained, not in a lethargic or debilitating way, more like a lightening up/freshening kind of feeling and I suddenly felt directed to climb into the sand dunes beside me.
There was a moment of hesitation but that passed and I turned and climbed the steep sandy slope.

As I got to the top I saw the head of a young girl begin to appear. She was sitting amidst the long grasses just back from the dune edge. As we made eye contact I smiled at her, and then noticed that she had a small pocket knife and was starting to cut at her wrist, a small dribble of blood beginning to flow.

I sat down beside her, and I don't think either of us spoke a word for a while. She didn't seem to mind me interrupting her, likely I expect she wondered where the hell I had come from, as you couldn't see the beach from that position, nor could she be seen from the beach.

I thought about telling her that the Holy Spirit had sent me to her, but I was well aware that such declarations are considered kind of nutty by those without a spiritual bearing.

So I sat there a while and then just asked her what was happening in her life. I recall that I didn't try to stop her cutting her wrist, which seemed odd, but I did not want to seem threatening to her or impinge upon her freedom to live or die as she chooses.

We sat there about half an hour, she stopped cutting and gave me the knife after a while. Some tears rolled and she related the victim's story of her manipulative boyfriend who wanted to control her and give up her life for him; a pretty common tale amongst young lovers.

I thought about trying to tell her how we choose our situations and that whatever happens to us is exactly what we need to happen to bring us to question 'reality'. I wanted to give her the whole universal theory about life but I didn't.
I instead started to tell her about the miracle center and what I did, about the other brothers there and how wonderful a few 'fresh 'ideas could be.

She seemed interested I thought, at least she wasn't running away, so we sat a bit and I told her about truth and illusion, duality, love and how I came to find her. Surprised that she hadn't put out rejection signals, I invited her for a coffee at the center where I hoped there would be those elder matriarchal figures milling about who could tend to the wound.

As we walked back to the miracle center she surprised me by saying that she used to think a bit like I did, but that the time with her boyfriend had squashed that free thinking in her and that she was keen to find her path again and be rid of him.

I bandaged her. We sat and had coffee. I gave her a twenty minute book, which we read page by page in turn aloud to each other, and she seemed to come back to life.

We laughed about the seeming misfortunes of life and the hidden opportunities to love and bless in each one, and after a lovely afternoon (*wherein I felt going to town no longer mattered*) we parted with a big hug, and I never saw her again.

About 6 months later I received a postcard from her in London. She was pursuing her dream of being a dancer and had joined a theatre troupe and was on the stage! I almost popped with joy.

INTEGRITY SINCERITY AND PRAYER

At several points during my transformation, at times when in asking through prayer for the healing of my mind in relation to heavily entrenched temporal concepts, I realized that I was lacking in sincerity.

My choice to stay true to the revelation of God was at direct odds with my desires for physical fulfillment and pleasures.

Yet in all things the Will of God is one will with mine, and so I knew that through asking for a miracle, (with no definition about that), things would align and I would be able to find the sincerity/integrity required to match the level of my ego arrogance and finally overthrow/vanquish these desires.

But as with all things, learning to fully accept my arrogances is the path to being able to release them. I realized I couldn't offer in prayer the shortcomings I was not fully aware of.

There's a line in the Course that says something like, "Everyone must come to look upon their anger and realize its full extent."

There were many times I glimpsed the tip of the iceberg but I had one moment in particular wherein I did indeed, with the help of the Holy Spirit, realize the full extent of my anger.

There is pretty much a basic list of emotional traits to being human. We don't have a wide variety of experiences despite our nationalities and cultures.

Jealousy, greed, envy, sloth, lust, wrath, pride, gluttony etc (the sins)… add to these the complexities of social wrapping, religions, science, education, government and relationships and there's a basic recipe for the ego's wrappings.

So at several points in my transformation's early years I found myself face to face with these ego traits, and on the one hand whilst I realized the loss of peace they caused me and my own failure to accept my shortcomings fully, I also realized that I needed to accept Atonement for myself in these instances and release my mind from the grip of guilt and hate that these human failings within me brought into my daily life.

I had a brief relationship with a woman at the center, wherein we were both in the recognition that the universe had somehow conspired to unite us physically for the unraveling of baser attributes and greater awareness of Self. Yet amidst the sexual/social background of the relationship I never paid a lot of attention to the nature of the relationship itself, although on many occasions it brought to me great stress and angst.

We split up many times over a twelve to eighteen month period, and at each interval I looked, but all too briefly, at the nature of the rift and its happenings, so that at about the fourth time it became apparent to me that something had to change if this relationship was to be transformed. But try as I may, I couldn't see what I was doing in the relationship that brought about these moments of separation. It was completely veiled from my awareness.

I realized that either I was going to end the relationship once and for all or I would heal it.

My integrity was challenged and I wouldn't stand for it. My decision was for peace - God, and I was determined to heal the rift rather than to carry my shortcomings into subsequent relations with others.

I had no way of knowing how this veiled sin, (*sin is an Aramaic archery term meaning 'Off the mark'*), was effecting my everyday life with others in other human interactions and I was determined to find the sincerity required for the hearts prayer to root out this within me.

Realizing that I had failed to do so on at least four other occasions with this woman, I determined that I would go and speak to her and ask her to join me in prayer.

I recall she seemed a little surprised by my request. But regardless, we decided to do it, and I asked her to come with me to the beach across the road to pray, in a kind of ceremony I guess. Something I felt I needed to do to try and even 'feel' sincere about the whole thing.

So we went and drew circles in the sand and I knelt in mine and was still a moment, trying with all my heart to feel/find that one moment of 'getting in touch' with my heart.

I recall I uttered a bunch of prayer like words, and at some point sensed a 'moment', which always to me feels as if the prayer has just taken flight from me and soared into the heavens.

I recall that she seemed a little uneasy about the whole ceremonial side of it and simply uttered amen. We returned to our respective homes.

I don't recall much about that relationship, other than that it ended on one level that night, but that it was definitely 'righted' in me and I was free of whatever it was that held me to the bondage of its cause and effect insanities.

I have drawn circles in the sand on several occasions when integrity for prayer seemed lacking, but at each time I have been somewhat spontaneous, not wanting to format any kind of set approach to God.

God to me is the creator, as part of that I consider the relationship to be on the one hand a singular happening, but also I have learned not to trust my ego and that whilst I find myself in a dreaming dimension/paradigm, I should approach my relationship with the Creator from that perspective and be undefended by a bunch of spiritual platitudes and rhetoric etc.

At one point, in dealing with the upcoming situation wherein I was being called upon to get rid of my dog from the center, I again found myself feeling called to find strength and integrity of prayer for help.

I was very attached to cobber and had raised him from a pup. He was a smart and well trained dog who had had many great 'boys own' style adventures with me in our country place just prior to the center days. Again I found it necessary to go alone to the beach, draw my circle and pray for strength to let go of my attachments to him.

Several days later I realized a shift in my thinking about the dog and not long after that a one legged man appeared who needed him more than me.

At the moment of giving Cobber up, it wasn't as difficult as I imagined. I missed him a bit, but every time I tried to access thoughts about him, they diminished more and more in emotional intensity.

Much the same shift has occurred for me in my ideas of sex, money, health and pretty much every concern of temporal association.

Another point of transformation/integrity was triggered one afternoon during a sudden upwelling of fear surrounding an idea that came to mind strongly of burning to death.
I had no clue where that thought came from, but it stuck fast and I realized that I was attached to the idea, it was my idea.

As nothing comes unbidden in this world I realized my responsibility to the idea as a part of my own consciousness story, and I resolved to confront the idea and expose it fully.

Up until my declaration to do this, I realized I had been trying to hide/subdue the thinking for my fear of the power of the thought to bring me loss of peace.

In those days I was new to transformation and often made physical confrontations with my fears, rather than allowing them as 'ideas' to be exposed and healed miraculously in the light during a light session/meditation which in essence, is an act of living prayer.

So not wishing to expose my fear of burning to death to others, I resolved to have a fire ceremony and allow myself to confront the fear as however it showed up. I had absolutely no clue what I was doing. I went to the far end of the beach and started collecting dried driftwood and sticks into a pile, dug a small pit to shelter the base from the winds and set a fire that would be large enough to cook a pot meal on.

After sitting beside the fire and allowing my mind to surrender to silence, I asked for Divine help to undergo whatever was required of me to overcome or release this fear.

I drew a long burning stick from the fire and holding it at one end, laid the burning end across my other arm. My arm did not burn. I recall being somewhat bewildered and again laid the stick across my arm, it burned that time.

The story of Moses asking God for water twice came to mind, I remember laughing at myself and went home to run cold water on my arm which to this day, still bears the 'Have Faith" scar.

But my fear was gone. Burning alive was like a small snail in my garden, whereas before it was a dinosaur. Nowadays it is nothing at all. The death/demise of the physical vessel is not something I care about. I am neither for nor against, for it simply exists to serve.

There's a line in the Course that states, "You must look upon your anger and realize its full extent." Theoretically I understood that the ego's goal is total annihilation of God, the universe, everything, including itself, but having that understanding as a concept and knowing it as my own horrific experience of false identity is two different things. Talk is cheap! End.

A Blessing

I had drawn the attentions of a woman at the center, who had for several years made comments, left odd presents/gifts and generally 'creeped' around in my conscious awareness as an idea of some crazy person who wanted a physical interaction with me.

I don't seem to recall having any immediate feelings toward this person (*for or against*) and her attentions did not really seem to register on any alarming scale in my mind.
She was no more to me than One in Christ on a good day (*during transformations trials*) and no more than an odd person to be blessed on a bad day.

But little by little and with increasing comment from others at the center I began to notice her attentions with ever increasing regularity. And it began to get under my skin!

Over the coming days it became apparent to me that she was 'stalking' me or some such thing. As I had been reading that line/section in the Course (You must face your anger and realize its full extent) several times during that period, I was even more aware/attuned to a higher level of vigilance regarding arising anger.

I was aware that the common perception of enlightened persons was that they no longer felt ego emotionality and lived in a kind of blissful state of being. I longed for this to be true but realized that absolutely every one of them had to undergo the purification of the ego and that I was going to have to as well!

A week or so later, there was a working bee at one of the brother's houses. Several brothers were living there at that time, including me. There was painting, cleaning, gardening and all manner of jobs to do as you would expect after just purchasing a multi bed roomed property on acreage.

On the day, about twenty brothers turned up from the healing center and set about the task of addressing the long list of jobs. I assigned myself to the restoration of the swimming pool paving, which was being upturned by the roots of a large tree nearby.

Everyone was working hard and it was a hot day. I think the pool paving was perhaps the hardest job on the list and I was all sweaty and had removed my shirt to try and find some escape from the heat. I recall seeing this woman around several times that day, but each time she was not working but staring bug eyed at me!

She came out from the house several times with a pitcher of water for all of us who were working under the sun and each time I became aware of her I was also aware of the 'gazes' she was giving me. I could feel my disdain rising…

To say I was not physically attracted to her was fact. She was not only not my type physically, but neither mentally. I recall her once dressing in adult baby clothing with a large teddy bear in town. It didn't bother me at the time as everyone just accepted her as 'different'.

But this day I was having trouble accepting that difference, and was feeling the upwelling of anger towards her (*which was actually towards my-self, projected outward in denial of my true power.*)

As I had previously seen this anger 'bubble' in me, I had spent an earnest session in private prayer to the Holy Spirit to expose my anger fully and I recall I prayed, that no-one would be hurt if my terrible anger surfaced for healing. I had become aware that the full extent of my anger could kill. It scared me what may come of my prayer but I placed all faith in God it would be perfect.

It was just after lunch and I had returned to the task of leveling the paving around the pool. All of a sudden I looked up at the pool gate and there she was, leaning doe eyed on the fence, staring at me intentionally like a hopeless teenage lover. It made me feel sick.

I erupted, casting an awful insult across the pool area and storming off past her across the lawn area towards my room. To my surprise she followed me across the lawn, taunting me, accusing me of hatred, telling me I wanted to kill her.

Then she started repeating 'hit me, hit me' over and over again. I could feel her at the back of my neck, anger was welling up and

I couldn't stop it. As we approached the entrance to the house I whirred around and hit her hard, knocking her off her feet mid-sentence. She fell heavily to the ground.

As I strode off, I looked at her slumped against the doorway and knew in that one instant that if I had been holding a knife she would have been dead. There it was, my desire to kill, anger in its unrestrained form fully exposed.

In that instant however was the accompanying awareness of purpose'. There was a 'moment', not born of time, the briefest of instants wherein I 'felt' or sensed an intercession of pure clarity.

It was as if I was outside my body looking in, witnessing the moment through a forgiven viewpoint. I knew instantly that my anger had been lifted from me.

It's funny and at the same time difficult to describe living without anger now. On one hand I am still able to react to situations that would have normally aroused anger, but it happens differently.

It is as if the script of my life has been edited somehow. It's the same act, the same characters, but a different perception and expression.

I have a deep sense of assertiveness and defenselessness where once anger would have brought me to conflict. I am occasionally told that I am kind of scary, that my power/assertiveness is unnatural.

My dear Ones that know me best often liken me, my energy now to that of the ancient biblical figure Moses, calling up to God to part the sea. I guess I look at the analogy with a sense of humor, finding it a bit difficult to pinpoint any association of myself with temporal figures, past or present.

I am often perceived by many eastern taught western minds in the spiritual community as someone who doesn't practice what he preaches. I am often seen to be a rough diamond to these types of white clad devoted ones.

They do not yet understand that being truly free means also that judgment of one's self, good or bad does not apply, and that the stereotypical image most western spirituals cling to of the cushion sitting serene figure is a vastly misunderstood notion.

The true master of spirituality is completely unconcerned and unapologetic of his actions, knowing that no matter appearances, Gods' will is done, separation does not exist.

This often brings a mind to re-examine its ideas about God. The human loves to put God into a manageable form, attributing sensibility, good relations and reciprocity to the expression of that considered divine.

It is not so, love is all encompassing and its expression in this world can manifest as any scenario, and does!

Learning to finally accept this releases the mind from all judgment. This is a step to take that many sincere spirituals balk at.

They cannot perceive of living beyond this point, with no roadmap for expression.

It seems to them that if they cross this line into unconditional acceptance, leaving behind all notion of how they are perceived by other spirituals or the 'aware/awakening' communities they gather to that they will be lost to some form of internal anarchy, the very thing they began spiritual work to escape.

But it cannot be escaped, not by meditation, not by ritual nor even death. Once the world is accepted exactly as it is however, inclusive of all its self-destructive and violent parameters, it ceases to disturb the mind, returning a full sense of inner peace.

Of course, as with the example I have mentioned in this section, each collapse of the minds peace signifies yet another parcel of denial, another corner of the minds basement that requires healing through forgiveness/acceptance.

To end this tale, the woman wrote me a beautiful letter of self-aware content, apologizing for the unwanted attentions and inner conflict it had roused in me.

I of course was grateful to her for being willing to have played such a powerful role for me to finally purge anger from my mind and I let her know it, with kindness and mercy, a joyous gift to have indeed.

LIGHT SESSIONS

Light sessions:

It is difficult to describe light sessions as in the main the experience they bring is of a divine nature and happens internally. There are though many and varied physical phenomena associated with them that can be discussed, but in all things, such discussion is pretty much pointless as experience is *always* the teacher.

In my own experiences during my light sessions I have had so many varying/transitioning reactions as I progress through my transformation that a starting point is tricky to recall.

Directly after my enlightenment in 1997 I attended the healing center only on weekends as I lived an hour and a half away and had to work three days a week.

It was not until I ran into one of the other brothers from the center at the Channon market that during the course of our conversation wherein she told me I had the energy of a dead fish, that I decided I needed to relocate in order to attend the center full time and undergo purification to 'true up' to what had been revealed to me in my enlightenment experience.

My mind was awash with the chaos of trying to reconcile the notion of two lives, one eternal and one physical. I had been trying to read the 'Course' back in my tipi, (I had moved onto the commune as an attempt to further divest myself of physical distraction, renting out my house which was nearby), but no electricity or light to read by at night and a very busy self sufficiency lifestyle during the day left me no time to study.

So after much discussion with my parents, who owned the house, it was decided to sell it and I would move to Byron Bay to attend my church full time.

From the very beginning it was a complete shift in my daily life. Not only was I to become vegetarian, but I also had to give up alcohol, cannabis and cigarettes.

I had given up alcohol immediately after my enlightenment however (*without any chagrin*), and even in that it was as if the enlightenment itself had fulfilled that within me that used alcohol to cope with my inability to find meaning.

At that time though, I was still using cannabis after dinner to help me get to sleep, without which I would often lay awake up to three hours before I could doze off.

But as with all things divine it was by pure Grace that I instantly gave up cannabis and meat and began my time at the center. I didn't know when I began, how long I would be there and when I asked within one time I was shown a graph, the time would be six years. And it was.

There were other marker points on the graph too, but it has been seventeen years since then and I still don't really know what transitions they marked. I am not concerned either, as I know that Gods will is done in all things and that what happens to me is meant to.

As I began the awkward task of integrating into daily life at Byron Bay, it became apparent that there were very few there that I could actually talk to about my enlightenment and that any attempts I made to do so usually resulted in what I considered to be 'smart ass' spiritual replies.

I did have several seemingly important and relevant questions that recurred in my mind, that the answers to would make great sense of things to me or at least that's what I hoped. Little by little I realized that I did indeed get my answers, just not as I thought I might.

I was assigned a guide for the first few months, to help me through the initial settling in period and I set about doing the daily service requirements, cleaning mostly, at the center that were assigned to me when I was not attending sessions or a library class.

It was quite some time before it dawned on me that sessions were basically momentary ventures into the higher conscious region of the mind, to have what we termed a 'light experience'.

These ongoing experiences were accumulative in nature, being basically a form of divine repetition, re-educating/reminding the mind to seek its higher point of focus away from temporal distraction. The effect of these light moments was always joy, peace and laughter.

The body however, originally designed as a vehicle for learning in an experience of being separate from reality/God, would often react violently and uncontrollably, something that to outsiders would look very odd and often be quite confronting.

I recall many times when someone would just walk in off the street (we always had an open doors policy) and see what was happening and then hurry out again. It took quite an open minded perspective on life to actually be willing to look and listen without judgment, and greater again to actually join in.

As earnest progress is made through the workbook of 'A Course in Miracles', the mind begins to undergo shifts in consciousness, sometimes subtle and barely perceptible, but at other times quite profound.

I recall waking up one morning after completing lesson 12 the night before and realizing that I was not the same person I was when I went to bed that night. I couldn't put my finger on what had changed, but it was as if I was suddenly akin to a tiny white bird flying through a vast blue sky, whereas the night before my mind felt as if I was stuck deep in a warehouse full of boxes, with no way out.

My mind had shifted from one that was a 24/7 cacophony of random and often depraved chit chat, to one that was like the Buddha, perfectly silent, with the only thinking being the thoughts I used to talk with throughout my day.

This took me a few days to come to terms with, but I was thrilled about it and wouldn't go back to the old me for any money. I did notice however that the shift had also wiped out vast chunks of memory. But not being able to recall what those memories were, I decided to ignore my residual ego as it attempted to reconstruct my past.

The first year at the center was full on for me with phenomena. I should add that a phenomenon is cool, but it is nothing at all compared to enlightenment.

But on and on it went. Voices, lights and all manner of lucid dreams, interconnected mind moments with other brothers at the centre and getting flung about all over the place by unseen energy waves/bursts. My body went through hell physically, but as I progressed through the workbook it started to calm down somewhat.

My teacher would often laugh aloud to see me (and others) go through our transitionary moments and as with all illumined minds, he too was able to transfer direct light to those receptive and devoted to the path of 'A Course in Miracles' (as I now am able to do in various regards also), which would seemingly add to the already uncontrollable reactions that the activation of our own internal light would bring.

I recall that at one stage, for a period of almost four or five months, I would get massive spasms in my core, that would literally launch me from my chair if I was seated or propel me violently backwards, to see me flat on my ass some four or five feet from where I was standing.

As we did the light sessions in roughly standing concentric circles, it was not too long before the others there would make a point to keep clear from behind me during the light sessions.

At one stage I would gather cushions from the room and pile them behind me to break my fall. The pain in my coccyx would often be unbearable and at times I would fall down as often as twenty times a day.

My teacher joked that I should try falling up…which didn't help matters.

Every day would bring a cavalcade of phenomena during our light sessions, sometimes almost imperceptible, but usually quite raucous.

Connecting with another brother in mind was a favorite and mentioned in the course as one of the true effects of a miracle moment/Holy instant. During these moments it was apparent that the minds of all humans are actually joined, as one mind.

In the movie Star Trek, there is quite a good depiction of this, portrayed through the alien beings comprising the race known to humanity as the Borg.

This experience, which would manifest in various ways without warning, at any time of the day, in session or not would always bring to me a sense of wonder and amazement, reminding me over and over that I am only ever experiencing my Self, no matter who I seem to talk with or where I seem to go.

This 'singular' perspective of Self is of course how inner peace becomes lasting and manageable. Without that, being constantly reminded in a myriad of ways of the nature of singular reality, the draw and attraction of the physical egoic world is far too strong to deal with and continually stay awake to.

Anyway, I guess talking about it is a moot point without it being experienced. Most people I've talked to about it, assume wrongly, I am referring to some kind of ESP or extra sensory perception.

I recall an incident one morning during session wherein I felt strongly compelled to punch one of the other brothers who was standing directly in front of me. I had no emotion about it or him. It was as if somehow a previous arrangement had been made and this was the time it was to be executed.

He was a regular guy and enjoyed his spiritual endeavors. I guess I would say he was one of the more devoted brothers there.

I recall having a moment's hesitation at the growing inner guidance I was receiving to punch him. He had his back to me and as I released my resistances to the guidance I remember pulling back my clenched fist, taking aim at the center of his leather waist belt and making a brief judgment regarding the power of the punch.

I didn't want to hurt him, but somehow I sensed the punch should be firm and solid. I let fly, landing a hard hit directly on his belt at which he let out a loud gasping "uurghing" noise.

Simultaneously, without me being prior aware of it, both women standing to his immediate left and right also lurched heavily backwards, letting out similar noises. Both these women had had intimate relations with him over different periods. All connected. All one.

Laughter in perfect unison was also an everyday occurrence during light sessions. I recall reading in the New Testament where Jesus describes heaven as the sound of children's laughter. I had endless experiences of minds joining during 'fits' of laughter. This was often accompanied by the experience of groups of devotees getting 'moved' together around the room as one group by unseen forces.

To say that the devotees were in a kind of trance would be a fair comment, but at all times fully aware of all things, a true union moment.

There are many tales I could relate about the light sessions, light flashes, haloes, angelic sounds, visions and revelations. But they would take a long time to talk about and would only really end up being food for the ego. It loves to build phenomena based identities, but without actually seeing through the illusory nature of even these things, keeping the experience of absolute truth/enlightenment at bay.

There's a whole world of spiritual gobbledygook out there. Some say it has its place to lead the aspirant further on but at what price. Time is always against you. Why waste it on crystals and tarot and all those other circular pastimes claimed as 'something' in the new age/quasi spiritual world of 'seekers'?

All those things only ever have the meaning YOU give them. Accordingly one's power, once invested in them, will manifest according witnesses to the validity of the beliefs. Yet it is still all temporal based, and therefore still just as meaningless as going to work at a factory or office etc.

If you want to find truth, you have to either draw your circle in the sand, or reach the point of no return. Even light sessions, as powerful as they are, can only ever give you glimpses of proof of God's existence.

It's the final decision/prayer of the heart for complete understanding and servitude that brings/triggers the inner code calling forth/earning enlightenment/salvation (freedom from reincarnation).

You can't fake that. You have to be truly done with the world.

"Give up the world and follow me." … (Jesus Christ)

My wife and I still host light sessions occasionally today, but things in my own/our personal transformation(s) have shifted a lot over 17 years although they are still as amazing and revealing as ever.

MAIN ST FADE

Declaration:

After several months, post enlightenment, I had just completed a three to four hour 'light meditation session' (for want of useful wordage), and was walking the fifteen to twenty minutes into town, where I would often go after sessions to have a coffee, chill out and get 'grounded' or something.

I was walking up Johnson St past the Focus gift shop. The street was really busy with people coming and going along the footpath. Being on a natural high from the meditation, I was in a superior kind of state of mind and as I wove my way through the crowds' oncoming, I had a thought...

"Wow, these are all my brothers"......

At which, the shops, street, and people all 'faded' like someone turning a dimmer switch and all I could see were tiny golden lights, where each person's third eye area would be I suppose. There was still a very dim glow of bodily shapes etc, in a grey blue hue...

I was shown that, no, these bodily things aren't your brothers. But these beings of light are!

Everything became the way it was again and I went and sat on the beach at the top end of the street to be with my vision, and let sink in what had just happened.

Peace

SUE

Introduction:

Every encounter on a spiritual journey is an encounter with your "self." You will either recognize in any given situation complete peace and acceptance of the situation as it presents itself in which case there will be virtually no observation/judgment of the situation.

Or, the situation will show you your own denial of love and peace which will show up as conflict or judgment of your own mind. As you become more aware of the mastery and application of the spiritual principles of your chosen journey you will become more attuned of the subtle energies that are always around you that you have trained yourself to take for granted; and miss.

Each moment in time every relationship you enter into no matter how small and trivial, or overwhelming and all-encompassing has a gift to hold out to you.

The following story is the documentation of a gift that was given to me through my experiences in Tilba Tilba with the funky crew who gathered together for a moment in time to undergo spiritual transformation through the application of the principles of 'A Course in Miracles'.

Sue:

The Miracle Centre in Byron had received a call from a woman called Sue who lived in Tilba several hours south of Sydney. She had picked up one of the little blue books we distributed around

Australia and was on our list of people to visit on our across the center Miracle Tour.

She had called the center prior to our departure, "I've got this little blue book here. It's speaking the truth. I want it. I want to do the whole thing. Can you come here? There are others here too ..."

It was that sort of a call, excited and fast. When Christine called to inform me of the call I knew inside that this was part of my assignment.

Luke, Cyena and I stopped in there on our journey for a few days and put on a workshop, for want of a better term. (*I am not keen using commonly bantered term as they tend to have loaded meaning and reference to the meaningless merry-go-round of new age stuff littering the western minds comprehension of spirituality*).

A few of the winter doused crew that showed up actually claimed to have a few experiences during the active meditation sessions we did and all in all I figured it went ok.

All three of us were new at this God stuff then. Outside of the sanctuary of the center in Byron we had no real way of knowing what exposure other communities may have had to the uncompromising auspices of the Course in Miracles or the stuff that we did.

When we finally arrived back at Byron, having had a grand adventure across Australia, there was a message waiting from Sue. "Would you please come back to Tilba, we have a meditation room set up for 'A Course in Miracles', and we want to do it full on, bla, bla, bla, love Sue and the gang."

A week later, Gina and I loaded up 'Miracle One" (*my old trusty Toyota van, which blows more smoke than a Nimbin pot festival*) and headed off on another twelve-hour road trip back to the sleepy little hollow of Tilba.

Tilba is a funny place, populated by rednecks and hippies and a smattering of old devotees who all seem to live in big houses on acreage hidden in the hills around the village. I guess there are only a few hundred residents of Tilba in all and I get that they like it that way. The place is heritage listed with a building cap.

Gina had come almost all the way with me on the Miracle Tour. She'd replaced Luke in Adelaide, who had done a short stretch from Byron to Adelaide before the 'I miss you more' pangs of his new relationship kicked in and he decided he had to go back.

I don't recall the trip back down to Tilba, but it was Gina's maiden voyage there and she was excited to be meeting Sue and the guys, as was I. It was really more that we were in the expectancy of more miraculous happenings, more minds popping.

Gina and I rolled up Sue's country drive way at about seven pm. Sue was in the kitchen and we were met with a great big country smile and a bit of that beholding kind of attitude that so many seekers carry with them so as to be noticed for how devoted and spiritual they are.

Part of me shivered inside but I think I hid it well enough. We had just driven twelve hours. I didn't want to be putting our hosts nose out of joint just yet.

Hot coffee, standing up and some cordial small talk would do fine for the moment.

But heck, who am I kidding, I knew that wouldn't last much past polite introductions and warm embraces. I was a bull in a china shop and I knew it, plenty of the guys at the center in Byron specifically avoided talking to me because of my reputation for rapier retorts. Conversation was definitely not my forte. You either wanted to wake up or not, don't bother me if not!

Sue bustled about making us some snacks and coffee and spoke enthusiastically about the last visit I paid her with Luke and Cyena.
One thing led to another and it wasn't too long before I got to asking her why she wanted us there. Of course there was no cutting answer. There rarely is in this business. Just around the bush outburst of immaturely expressed spiritual desires based on scantily understood spiritual concepts.

I already knew why she wanted us there of course, but I wanted to see if she knew. It would be a lot easier if she already had some idea of what she was getting into, then I didn't have to be the bad guy, just someone who reinforces what she already knows. She had no clue.

On the first trip to Tilba I never got to speak to Sue at length. The hubbub of the workshop occupied most of my time answering questions and comforting the egos of those who unwarily found themselves faced with the shocking facts of self-confrontation.

"I want to embrace blah, blah God, blah, spirit, blah and blah." She was really soft and squishy nice in those days, one of those super nice spiritual identities who hasn't yet realized they don't exist, and doesn't want to. Sue is a lot different today, she has balls.

"I will do anything you say." She says to us, smiling meekly, not quite sure if that was the best thing she could have said, but to me that was exactly the best thing she could have said and I knew what it was that I was going to get her to do.

Sue has a huge head of long black curly hair, which dropped, almost to her waist, completely at odds with the Buddhist accoutrements, which adorned every ledge, shelf and wall of the big country house.

"Well good," I replied, "being willing to do whatever it takes is the whole thing, giving up the world being the whole thing."

She looked straight at me in the same sort of way parents do if a police officer comes to the door asking the whereabouts of their child.

"Let's begin with losing all that hair." I said, half bracing myself for what may follow. Silence . . . . Stares at Gina, stares at me, mouth drops open, half a laugh, a stutter and all hell broke loose in the kitchen. I had touched a sore point, it's easy to say that you are willing to give up the world, but actually getting around to doing it by even so much as a haircut . . . you gotta be shittin' me.

Well she ranted about all sorts of spiritual stuff, all types of reasons why that couldn't possibly be something she had to do, "I did that before, I'm not a Buddhist blah blah blah."

The simple fact of the matter was however that I had asked. It was a symbolic expression of an offering I was making her to enable her to come to a new greener pasture, quieter waters.

From the moment I began to take in the house, her style and the general feel of the place, it was clear to me that I had walked smack into the external representation of my own denial, showing up as what I used to think being spiritual was all about. Incense, books, candles, Buddha statues etc . . . it made me feel ill.

I could have simply taken a moment and laughed at myself and walked out, job done, the spiritual path is not about others per say, as there aren't any others, only reflections of my own denial (ego) or the Christ.

This was not Christ I was seeing and I wasn't going to try to deny that I had a negative reaction to the whole scenario. It truly did make me want to upchuck.

There are two ways of dealing with denial of Christ/ God - in the form or in mind.

In mind is immediate, a lot more discreet and has almost no whiplash save the odd tears/laugh session. In the form is a little trickier and takes longer, but either way, cause and effect are never separate and I was having a grand time watching the show unfold this way, and hey . . . there's no right way or wrong way to do this, no set blueprint. Everyone has to work out their own salvation, me included.

What could I do? There was this thing asking for help, who assured me she wanted to help others, which I knew she would be good at, *(which is the only thing that stopped me leaving)* and the only help that came to mind was a haircut.

I rifled through the kitchen draws sensing the scissors there and sure enough a lovely pair of tortoise shell handled choppers emerged which fit the bill nicely.

Sue's eyes widened as the reality of my sincerity dawned. Had she said no problem to the whole thing then I would not have continued with the whole thing and her hair would likely be to her butt by now, but there was more underground resistance to the idea of a haircut than there was in France with the Nazis during WW2. The hair had to go and that was final.

The final surrender came when I assured her that Gina and I would not compromise and that we would get straight back in the van and go all the way back again if she had only gotten us down here to accept what we stood for on her own terms.
I love that scene in the matrix when Neo has the gun in his face and the girl says "It's our way or the highway." This was that scene. Instead of a gun there was scissors.

Gina was great; she backed me up all the way. When Sue tried to get her on side with the ole' 'We girls gotta stick together routine.' she stood firm in her non-compromising approach to just this sort of situation and said calmly.

"This is a gift Sue. It's not just what you think it is and I am with Dave on this." Boom. After a little more nervous tension, a lot of "Oh god, oh god", and a bit more disbelief, the locks fell heavily to the floor. I ain't no barber but I think I did a fine job, collar length, round, no pokey bits . . . .

Sue died there in the kitchen that night; at least her ego did, pretty much anyway. She sobbed and laughed in that disbelieving way that people do at the news of tragedy . . . and she shone. There was suddenly a new thing standing there in the kitchen, a whole new energy belonging to a whole new association of beings, the light was in.

Whether she knew it or not, Sue had a haircut by Jesus that night, one that came with all the trimmings of the Salon Divine, humility, honesty and integrity.

That was a night fit for the Akashic records, and we all knew it, and despite that she was some few moments getting used to it, Sue was truly grateful. All said and done it was really only hair and meant nothing, none of it did in truth, but that's the journey, it's often faced in form in the beginning, until the students mind learns to make the shifts internally. I like that part, it's like a grand homecoming production, and we all laughed a lot that night. Bloody good stuff.

We stayed there for a few weeks, putting on sessions three times a week, attracting all the zombies and dead things out of the hills to come hear of salvation and the path of self-healing, which is 'A Course in Miracles'.

I am not being rude here, anything which is not awake is asleep …. dead.

Remember Jesus' reference, "Let the dead bury the dead."

That's what he means, if you are not experiencing direct union with the divine, with eternal life, you are dead, asleep. If you don't know who you are, you don't know anything.

Everyone does know who they are really, but the amnesia of ego (*time space*) is completely obscuring and the process of breaking through to the other side of the veil can take a lot of chutzpah.

It's like we are all in a huge play, acting our parts, then I suddenly have this incredible divine dissolvement into God and come back some time later knowing the world is a sham and no one wants to believe me, preferring to stay oblivious to the fact of the matter that at a deep level of mind held in their unawareness they already know.

So here I am, awake amongst the sleeping, alive among the dead, seeing amongst the blind, it's almost more hellish than before I was awakened.

But back to Sue. A few days after the hair debacle, whilst Gina was having a nap, I was standing in the kitchen by the potbelly fire whilst talking to Sue through the open bathroom door. She was taking her nightly bath, a little ritual, which I disrupted sometime later, not really worthy of a bigger mention than that, no real tantrums.

As we spoke she expressed to me how truly grateful she was that we had come, and that she wanted us to feel free to do whatever we thought necessary to get things, energy moving.

Well, one of the things I know about Jesus is that he likes that things are simple and straightforward, uncompromising and clear.

He has no beef with anyone, other teachers, deities or the such, but if you want to get in his bus to heaven then you got to get on fully and not jump rides half way for a slower or prettier bus.

He has no time for the undecided, you go to get on hot or get on cold, but you can't get on lukewarm. No fence sitting.

Sue couldn't see me from the tub, and so whilst we talked I went about the house gathering up all the little wooden statues of Shiva and Buddha, Ganesha and whatever other deities I could find and started feeding them into the potbelly stove.

I loved doing that, and I loved the expectancy of the possible confrontation I supposed would follow when Sue discovered what I had done.

To add to the surprise, I took a golf putter and went around the garden outside and promptly knocked off all the heads of all the plaster and concrete Buddas there too.

Sheer delight! Back inside I stripped the walls of all the Papaji, Gangaji and other guru pictures and photos I could see and popped the glowing red belly of fire too.

I was on a roll now, I felt like an exorcist cleansing the Australian rural version of the Vatican of its myriad idols and meaningless treasures.

To me there was simply no Sue, only reflections of my own spiritual madness, staring at me from all sides.

The last identity to fall away before God is the spiritual one, in God no identity is possible at all, you already are what God created you to be (Spirit) and cannot bring any souvenirs of time space to the formless realm at all, no yoga moves, no incense, no beads, no kundalini dances, no rainbow songs, no philosophy, nothing.

Those who have shed the world have no use for anything from the world, religions, beliefs, accoutrements, no use for anything learned in the world at all, nothing.

Enlightenment leaves you very ordinary, very quiet, at peace with yourself. The transformational process is two parts however, the revelation AND the purification.

It can take many years to accomplish the journey, or perhaps just a few if you are truly earnest.

Death cannot exist - I Life. Darkness cannot exist where there is light. One cancels the other out entirely, and time cannot exist where there is only eternity.

"This house is clean." I declared to no one in particular, and retired to watch some TV, leaving Sue to soak a while longer before dinner.

Ten minutes or so later and I can tell Sue is in the kitchen in her robe putting on the kettle for a cuppa' before toddling off to her room to get dressed.

"Where is the picture of . . . .?" I hear her start to say, a moments silence followed whilst she registered all the other things that were there before she opened her big, relaxed, bath time mouth . . . the dream of separation is about to undergo another shift and I can taste it in the silence between her thought like when a car drives past you through a puddle and you can feel the cold wet water hit you just before it does.

I started to snicker inside, the interval was beautifully excruciating. I did not know if I could hold myself together much longer.
Then as if on cue; actually exactly on cue . . . . "Where are all my thing, the Buddha's and photos, everything . . . Daaavvviiid."

It was too late and she knew it. I strolled into the kitchen in silence and pointed to the glowing potbelly stove. "You didn't, you wouldn't . . . no you wouldn't, you . . . oh god, oh god."

Stove door opens, jaw drops, eyes go wide, stutter, stammer, a tear here, and a tear there. . . laughter.

I LOVE it when laughter happens, the mark of acceptance. Not so good when there isn't any laughter, but it's still all perfect, 'all good' as the popular Australian saying goes.

Sue was up front about the whole thing, and when she discovered all the smashed heads around the garden the next day I think that the mercury was tempted into rising again, but it went cool quickly.

Sue had a few days with me by then and although she didn't really understand my method, she knew enough to realize that she alone conducted the orchestration of my actions, I was only the medium by which the Lord worked according to her request for enlightenment.

True transformation never looks how you think it will, there are rarely nice squishy moments at the outset, more often there are a lot of short sharp shocks to get you dislodged from the rut of humanity just long enough to show you a glimpse of life without safety, without security, without all the zones and barriers we set ourselves up with to maintain our denial of God - keeping God to blame, in the image we would have him be in, and not as he truly is . . . no image.

The play out between Sue and I is really only an extreme or vivid example of a very individual beginning of her own awakening process, for me it represented an opportunity to stand firm knowing that I could do no wrong, that I was facing my own mind, being honest with my own observations and reactions, and letting the drama unfold as it may without defending myself.

I am the golden haired boy.

THE HIGH COUNCIL

The high council:

A few years into my time at the Byron bay healing centre I had come to the conclusion that I was under some kind of observation from minds already ascended from this realm, or something like that.

In the course of pursuing my enquiries about this idea I went to see one of the other teachers at the centre to seek further information about it, which was forthcoming in various regards, but unfulfilling of the depth of my enquiries.

There's a point when you just know that further enquiry into something is pointless and in this case I had not encountered that point so I decided to dig deeper.

I don't honestly know how I knew to do as I did, but I just found myself 'doing' it.

Late one evening after session, I guess maybe around eight pm, I found myself walking to the bathroom through the session room which was empty. I suddenly decided to arrange some of the white plastic chairs we sat on each day into a small circle in the rooms centre. It was a large room, like a conference room really.

I arranged twelve chairs into a tight circle, placed twelve cushions and decided to invite my holy guides to sit with me. I recall thinking it a bit odd to arrange chairs and cushions, but consoled myself that it was merely a symbolic act, defining my sincerity really.

I stood in the centre of the circle alone and spoke aloud to Jesus. I don't recall exactly what I spoke but I expect something along the lines of "Show Yourselves . . ." (*don't ask me where the idea came from, madness I expect*)

At that time in my process I was often referred to as "Moses", having a kind of raw biblical style energy. Others referred to me as a bull in the china shop. Either way, that was me, completely 'burned' from the experience of Enlightenment and oblivious to all personal boundaries, political correctness and social expectations etc.

At one point during my circle I was interrupted by one of the elderly matriarchal figures that often attempted to promote and keep some kind of spiritual order to things at the center, but I was having none of that.
As she attempted to tell me that "We don't do such ceremonies etc. at this center…" I laughed aloud, ignoring her and carried on talking to Jesus aloud regardless.

She wandered off muttering under her breath, leaving me to conclude my prayer/appeal in peace.

After a short while I returned to my cabin after locking up the center for the night and tucked myself into bed, laying there watching TV. After turning the TV off I lay in bed staring a moment out the glass door into the night outside. All of a sudden I became aware of a small golden sphere, translucent and glowing, hovering in mid-air about two meters from my bed, about two feet from the ground, level to my face.

As I lay there looking at the sphere, I recall feeling warmth inside me and a sense of deep calm. All of a sudden the sphere came slowly over towards my face, grew very large in size and engulfed me, at which I was once again, for the second time, 'gone' from the physical realm.

I once again found myself bodiless, pure mind. I recall trying to look down to see if I had a body but couldn't. I was awareness, mind... but this experience/dimension I was now in was completely different to being one in the Godhead.

This experience still had a kind of dimensionality about it, though I can't satisfactorily explain it despite my many attempts over the years.

I was in a kind of ephemeral amphitheater surrounded by what I can only describe as 'elders' or 'higher beings'.

As my mind/I, became more aware of them, one of them 'floated' down/over to me and took me round the circle, making it somehow clear to me the nature of the 'higher order' of beings I was now in the presence of.

As we passed from one to the next I noticed a gap. Sensing my awareness of the gap, I was told wordlessly, "This is where your teacher Ted sits." At which point I exited the experience and found myself back in my bed in my cabin.

I immediately dressed and raced over to Ted's cabin and told him what had happened. He told me "Cool, you likely just got your assignment."

I recall thinking that his response was somewhat indifferent and went home soon after feeling a little flat, kind of as if I was expecting some Ta Da' moment between Ted and I.

Over the next few days/weeks, information I didn't realize I had surfaced into consciousness and I found myself thinking it was likely time to pack my van and start taking 'A Course in Miracles', to Australia at large. Which, after a few months I did.

The moment I was to do that dawned on me during session one day soon after, whilst sitting on a table at the side of the room listening to Ted talking about the Course.

I heard Jesus speak to me directly, clearly, saying simply, "Dave, you're done."

At which point Ted looked over at me mid talk and said, as if to confirm my internal instruction, "Dave, you're done."

It was still a few months till I raised enough cash to set off, but I eventually departed the centre for a round Australia trip with two other crew and several boxes of books, making our way southwards, and around the great Australian bight across the desert to western Australia and back again. But that's another story!

THE JOGGER

Several years after my enlightenment after a particularly deep meditative morning, I was walking the beach as I often did to be 'alone' with my emerging/maturing spiritual thoughts...

The beach was deserted, which I considered odd, as there were usually people about at that time of the day, even if only a few.

I recall thinking that there weren't even any joggers, which was especially odd as there were always joggers.

There was not one person on the beach in front of me as far as the eye could see.

All of a sudden, a man materialized about one hundred meters ahead of me, jogging, red shirt, sneakers, heading straight towards me. As if a slit had opened in time and he had stepped through it in that instant.

I recall thinking/knowing, that if I had stopped him, he would have had a name, family life, full story, as to his existence on earth, although he had not existed before I made him up.

As I turned and watched him jog off toward Byron Bay town, I was aware that I felt somehow un-amazed ... as if I knew somewhere in my mind perfectly well that I was making this whole thing up...

Peace

TODAY

Today - 11/9/14:

Today, at the time of writing, I am physically 49, almost 50 years. My desire level for things of the world is minimal.

Sex seems to be the thing people get most hung up on after all other concerns of mortal life are faded through transformation.

And certainly sex seems to have faded drastically almost entirely from my agenda of temporal delights and I am happy for it to continue to do so.

Sex is our basic survival mechanism of course. It is raw and primal, existing to 'make' more of us in separation, just as 'giving or extending" is creation's expression in eternity.

Like all things transformed, it doesn't matter whether you do it or don't do it, own something or don't own it... only that it has no value to you.

Things are merely useful or not. Used until they are not, with a willingness to be in the constancy of letting go.

This takes honesty, and as I sit writing I imagine my honesty level to have exceeded my own comprehension of the idea, yet I am not foolish enough to entrust my own capacity alone as guide to make decisions by.

(There is a common misperception that an enlightened person lives ego free. This of course is impossible whilst maintaining a physical form, which is the very symbol of ego itself!)

As with every decision in transformation it must be made and guided through deferral to higher level mind, Holy Spirit *(I am that.)*

So recognizing Self/God and completing a thorough/irreversible process of temporal re-association is what awakening is.

Mind awake knows itself as whole, guiltless and free. It makes no excuse for itself and plays its part in the world without concern.

Today, I am that God-man incarnate. Prophet to some, visionary, teacher, healer, whatever is required each instant. Some hate me, regretting the day they set foot through my door. Yet in truth even the rigors associated with a minds unwillingness to accept every action/reaction, whether by the hand of an awakened mind or not are going to be the same rigors/energetic manifestations showing up in that person's life in one way or another. Karma is inescapable!

I consider that the benefit of confronting ones karma in the association of an awakened mind is simply that there is an availability to learn from the experience, rather than to regret or recoil from the opportunity to go beyond current learning awareness of Self.

The rigors imposed by various sects of the Hindu (and Sufi faiths) through the supplication/surrender to a Sadhu/Guru are a good example to take into account. Anyone considering seeking out a teacher should likely be aware that a good teacher will do absolutely anything to help you confront and accept your limitations/chains…even unto your death.

These days I have little concern/interest for the majority of students in the ACIM world, who in the main I consider to have been led by various smiling self-anointed gurus into circular factions of mind/time wasting conceptual comfort groups.

Most desire no more than to learn the basics of this application that they may attempt a 'higher' sense of living, to have a better life in the world.

There are few indeed who want to leave the world entirely. But unless complete liberation is the goal, application of spiritual principles will lead but to a faster path to death, (also perfect, but no one needs help for that, death and reanimation on the physical plane is certain for all who sleep, dreaming of awakening.)

Atonement doesn't require my physical presence, yet it is useful a moment longer in this Holy path whilst time/space lasts. I never know when the next bold explorer, risk taking aspirant of truth may grace my door, this truly is my prayer of gratitude.

If you have awakened and have no clue what has happened to you, reading this book now I urge you to the workbook of 'A Course in Miracles'.

If you are in a recognized (by you) process of awakening/transformation I also urge you similarly.

As declaration I should also add that to use the wording I have in these documents is obviously a dualistic expression, me and you, separation, no one can avoid it in time/space.

The singular nature of Self has, however, left me with a profound appreciation of 'All is One' as my own internal recognition, which is automatically applicable in those moments of transformation wherein any loss of peace, no matter its reflected externals, comes to bear.

To say the peace of God is shining in me now is an understatement of gross proportions, I AM that!

What is written on these pages will and is completely meaningless to me now, yet I recall that at one time I would have given my last breath to find collaboration with my journey' in such a form, something to help make a bit of sense of what was happening to me.

There was, is and will never be any authority in this world that can help you awaken except another awakened mind, or your own fearless and/or foolish efforts to countenance insanity.

So, do whatever comes to you in salvation, go wherever it leads, outward or inward and let it lead you into light and dark. If you feel you need to seek me out then do so. But know I cannot fill a cup already holding water. I am always with you.

Our place at Avatar (Mackay, Queensland, Australia) is open to all earnest travelers.

We are developing Avatar into a resource and learning center for those both curious of life's meaning and those already completely uprooted by the spiritual journey. We also are grateful for all help given.

Avatar will not be the *first* center of its kind in Australia, but as the old center is now closed it will be the only current one! Peace.

Avatar
Po box 11114 Canelands,
Mackay QLD, 4740 Australia.
Phone: 0401442200
        0417200331

TRANSFORMATION

Transformation post enlightenment:

There are many people I've met, post enlightenment, who have experienced light and or phenomena to such a degree that their lives are forever changed, as mine was.

The difference between us as temporally activated entities is that I count myself lucky enough to have been activated amidst surroundings of support through being in the company of so many 'A Course in Miracles' students.

I often wonder at the nature of enlightenment. It's seemingly happen chance particulars and the flotsam and jetsam it leaves of people's lives who seemingly stumble across it unprepared.

Whilst on one hand Gods' will is total, it sure seems that the seemingly random nature of awakening and enlightenment is something that no blueprint was ever drawn for.

The levels of mind, those ascended minds, overseers of salvations particulars (whom I call the council) are definitely aware of who is where/ready for what and how it all goes together, but I can't help but thinking that the light workers on earth are wholly integral to their functioning, and we are barely scratching the surface in many parameters.

But it goes on, and to date I seem to be the only one I've met in salvations path who has had the level of experiences I have had, enlightenment/no world included. Of course there's many I've met who profess similar experiences, but the experience of the truth is identical for all, being an experience of total oneness, a singularity.

Each person's story of their spiritual experiences has been somewhat different to mine and I can only put that down to the fact that it is MY dream, so naturally it is only to me to whom such an experience should need to happen. I can hear the gnashing of the teeth of minds who consider themselves contemporary to me at that statement, but all arrogance aside its true.

I met a chap in Brisbane who used to practice some kind of meditation. Something he put together himself as a result of many years of involvement with various yogic classes.

He was deep in meditation one day and all of a sudden slipped between the moment of conscious awareness into the 'void', that place between consciousness and light'.

But instead of being shot back to consciousness, he found himself beside a lake of gold, in a different place wherein all things and beings were golden light. This is similar to my experience, except that I found myself directly AS light, there were no bodies, forms, world …nothing but light, me as light and the light as me.

This lake of gold experience unlocked an awareness of 'other' dimensions, places wherein we can exist, but are perhaps somewhat 'ahead' of our journey for now.

For this man it was intolerable, to be stuck with a mortgage, family and life of duality, on earth, knowing there is an alternative, that can be reached, but not maintained, with no apparent way to attain it.

I recall sitting with him several times over some years, we would talk about 'A Course in Miracles', spirituality, life and stuff, but our talks would always come back to his dilemma.

He hadn't slept for periods of 3 months or more, many times, and the last time we met his eyes were red and swollen around, his complexion pallid and drawn and his demeanor that of a man losing a long fought battle.

As I tried in vain to attempt to get him started on the workbook lessons of the Course, it became clear that the story of hopelessness he had spun himself had a stronger grip on his mind than he knew, and that my efforts were in vain. He could not hear me, he was fried.

As I left him for the last time, driving off in my van, it occurred to me that he was me, at least a version of me (me being everything/a singular idea of Self) that was a reflection of my potential, what could have happened to me had I not availed myself of the brotherhood I was led to at the Healing centre in Byron. I realized that 'I' was the only one who needed to stay true to ACIM principles, to true up to MY experience/enlightenment, that everyone else was merely 'versions' of me, actors, playing out my potential/dream, as it would have been had I not begun my transformation proper.

Inwardly, I felt responsible for this man, for all those who play the suffering card, my heart bursts at times for those in the world not at peace. And then it comes back at me, "who is not at peace?" This is an illusion.

No one can live 24/7 in this realization; however it would indeed send u mad. The few minutes a day of doing the lessons in the workbook, and the moments wherein the chaos of human life brings your attention to snapping/application point is enough for most. For me the first few years was 24/7 however. As I said before, if not for the network of brothers at the Centre I would be lost. TYF (Thank You Father)

There are others I've met, saturated ones, those who have spent so much of their lives immersed in books and workshops and mystic travels in search of meaning, that the search has become the meaningful. The heavy barrage of over learned principles cross referenced religious dogma and ritual is a heavy curtain.

These too my reflections- meaningless thoughts circling, keeping alive the idea of a world apart from God.

Freedom of mind is also freedom from spirituality too.

I have several people a year turn up for something or other these days, mostly Course students or those who are feeling the drawings of the suicidal urge. The suicidal ones are usually good to work with as they have little if any pre conceived notions of anything spiritual, and with no options immediately apparent they have nothing to lose but I have no clue what they do with what they learn here in the main. Most just want a better life in the world and I don't teach that.

The Course students are mostly entrenched usually encumbered with years of searching and groups of every kind. It takes a lot to make a dent. But if they're willing enough, old dogs can be taught new tricks.

Learning that you are unwilling to surrender/listen within is mostly a shock to those claiming to be students/seekers etc..

Their whole arrangement is that they have certain egoic self-credibility in their path and are not all that keen if you don't validate their efforts (which I couldn't be bothered about).

I would estimate that within a group of ten to twelve students at least three to four will have some profound experiences early on and others at later dates when their 'realizations'/open mindedness comes to them through usually harsh and humbling admissions of self-denial.

Of course there's no exact blueprint of who is ready for what and who isn't but in general, just as there are a fairly open and plainly comprehensible association of principles and practices in spiritual work, there are also a fairly standard set of personality types too.

Not wanting to take away from the singular action in all this of course, the overriding principle of any spiritual work is the acceptance of Self in all things. Yet in order to write anything at all, it is required that duality is allowed to be set onto form and paper for a NEW purpose, realigning the thinking as it needs to be done. Were I to write this book from a singular perspective, it should have no pages at all, or least they would all be blank if it did!

I often offer the anecdote of Jesus in this situation; A man who knew himself to be Christ/minded without need to do anything but simply exist should he choose. But he did not choose that, he agreed to play a most vital role and teach the sleeping about salvation's call, right up to the crucifixion and beyond.

Certainly I am hoping my own ordeal will not have to extend to such parameters, but I can find no fear internally these days that would cause me angst if I should.

In the main the majority of us who embark upon the rigorous path of salvation to enlightenment (non-temporal experience) will have simple teaching and learning roles.

AH, and whilst I am on that note, beware anyone who attempts to charge you for lessons, offer you discipleship/stewardship courses and certificates etc… frauds!

They sound credible, quote all manner of teachings and spiritual accomplishment but have nothing to offer but words. Confront these charlatans for some kind of experience of direct light transference and watch them run or offer a jargon story.

Ask and ye shall receive' is the Christ minded credo. And it is not offered as a false gift. If you ask truly, then truly you shall receive. I have seen far too many miracles through my hands, and through the hands of others to know that what is promised by God is given to him who asks truly.

The one caveat to that is however, "Give up the world and follow me", asking for the sake of enhancing/healing your earthly lot/body is not in line with salvation's call. It's not that you won't receive your healing, but that your earth bound ego will quickly corrupt the purpose given to the gift/miracle and before long you will attract another disease/situation as before.

Once begun, the path of salvation cannot be turned on. It is a straight forward and confronting advance into the darkest places of your mind, as if entering a long dark tunnel on faith, and walking straight until finally light begins to appear at the other end.

Depending on passion, determination and willingness, that can be a short journey through the dark or a very long one indeed.

Those who claim the rainbows and butterflies version of spirituality are merely those who talk about it and assume that to do so and to associate with others who do so is what the spiritual journey is. These ones often have framed pictures of various Babas and Gurus adorning their walls, statues and icons of various sorts to declare their spiritual ideas of themselves to others.

This is so hilarious that I can barely refrain from laughter in such people's houses… well, yes I suppose that's a judgment, but in my job learning to laugh at illusions/my dream is the whole business. Perhaps this is why the Buddha was claimed to be a man of laughter, and why the sadhus of India are often referred to as wandering madmen. Some may claim me to be arrogant, but in my book not to realize the nature of illusions and to allow your beloved to sew themselves a trap of false identities is arrogance to me.

But if I were to use the example of Buddhism, the novice monks spend their days sweeping and chanting and tending various gardens and altars and it seems nice and happy to be doing something other than working hard for a living, but this is only the honeymoon period.

As time goes by, the monk soon confronts the tedious nature of even these once happy chores and enters into a more concentrated period of deep contemplation, and further into deep and terrifying practices that will consume his whole being, until he either reaches enlightenment or runs away from his monastic devotions.

TEACHINGS

A woman, the wife of a wealthy aristocrat, who had particularly white teeth, came to see the spiritual master. "Teacher," she sobbed, "My life is a string of social parties, wealthy friends and I have everything any woman could desire, yet within my heart I am insufferably unhappy and empty. I want to find God more than anything. Please help me."

The master, considering the woman's appeal, stroked his long grey beard and spoke to her , saying simply, "Go , and sell your body in the marketplace, abandon your life this very day and live among the poor and the wretched of life's people, there you will find what you are truly looking for."

One evening, four years later, the master had occasion to visit a sick child in one of the filthiest pars of the city. On his way to the home of the child, a woman of the night, bedraggled and gaunt, eyes like two dark caverns, but her smile, with teeth that sparkled ever so brightly, caught his eye.

"Hello there teacher," she spoke softly from the doorway.

"Hello child, I see you took my advice, and you have found what you were looking for." He said.

"Yes dear teacher, I have, and thanks and praise to God for you." she said.

"Tell me then," said the master, "why have you not returned to your husband, and your comfortable life?"

The woman started to laugh, and the teacher started laughing too, both already knowing the answer, which she so correctly uttered , "What difference would it make?"

ACTIVE PRAYER
(Why are their hands in the air?)

(This page is inserted simply as an attempt to explain the metaphysical nature of the "Light Sessions" we did at the Centre. It's very brief and there is much more could be told about them.)

I know it looks strange - people jumping up and down and people with their hands in the air. Unusual and unexplained behavior can often be frightening to those who do not know what is going on.

This behavior is simply a natural and uninhabited response to the joy and light of spirit. To be inspired is to be filled with spirit. You will not be left comfortless, and when you make Him welcome, the Holy Spirit shines His light into your mind. You become filled with an awareness of love that cannot be contained. You may find yourself literally jumping for joy!

That's all it is! It is nothing to be afraid of! The behavior that you see is nothing more than what you might call 'body language'. The body tends to express your state of mind. For example, if you are depressed or fearful, your body will tend to close up into a fetal position.

On the other hand, if you are feeling loving and joyful, your body will tend to open just as a blossom opens to the sun.

It is an expression of your willingness to give and receive.

If you allow the body to freely express love and joy, you may find that your hands are openly stretched above your head.

You are physically demonstrating an extension of that which has been given you. And, at the same time, your body is assuming a physical alignment with the light that comes from above.

While we encourage you to be free, we do not teach or require a specific behavior.

It is the action of your mind that is important. The Atonement is an act of Love, which is an inclusive extension of your mind.

Adjusting to the angst of time/space verifies its grip on the mind, encourages the universe to offer more of the same perceiving that what I want I get!

Collapsing karma by not adjusting to my emotional/mental irritations, accepting where/how I find myself, being still, breathing consciously and allowing my emotional reactive egoistic state to simply be healed/released through a willingness to forgive myself all things (non-implicit of guilt/blame) in an open minded recourse to source (spirit) for the reunification of single will directive purpose.

CONSIDERATIONS OF AN ENLIGHTENED MIND OF OUR TIMES

As I sit to write, having just read several articles in a recent philosophy publication, it comes to me that my own state of consciousness is somewhat restrictive in terms of associative ideas and comparative thought systems and may be little use in actually writing this now. However, inner guidance being the fall back overriding egoic concerns, I will continue until or if I hit a conceptual wall or paradox etc.

In my line of thinking/teaching, paradox is the place I guide all thought system application towards, except in this case it would be inappropriate as the purpose of this writing is as much to introduce myself to the world at large as it is to offer some small insight into the very nature of human limited consciousness itself, of which I am capable and able both to escape from at will and also teach others to do the same.

The scientific proof of this is only in application and with the exception of journalistic notations and scientific instrument measurement of brainwave activity and such, the actual witnessing to the jump from human limited consciousness to unlimited awareness of truth (and its subsequent ramifications) is only possible individually (although in group exercise it can be seen through effects.)

I think in the main the reason I am targeting the fields of psychology and philosophy with this writing is that, I have long witnessed that exponents of these arts tend to be like dogs chasing their tails.

There are so many minds going around expounding their various views and quoting classic and contemporary sources, but none who seems to be able to put it altogether to change the nature of their lives and more importantly, the lives of the general populous to bring about change to our invocation of purposeful ideas as a whole.

So in building an introduction, a doorway through which an individual, educated or not, can peer into my world, it dawns on me, I need a universal standpoint. This standpoint (a basic notion) must by nature then be all encompassing and accessible to anyone who wills to look as I do, at the nature of life, universe, everything!

The observer (the individual consciousness association) will do, but in order to begin to use this as a platform through which to effect change, it must first be understood what the observer is and more importantly, isn't!

To say 'I think therefore I am' is a pure limit on what the observer is. Naturally no sane mind will deny its ability to assume its 'living' status based on its examination of itself and its surroundings. The evidence for a correlative inner/outer spatial/mental reference is overwhelming and seemingly conclusive. There is virtually nothing bar the insertion of philosophical speculation that proclaims it otherwise.

Certainly the historical accounts of ascetics and illumined minds throughout the ages allude to paradigms beyond our contemporary grasp as a whole. Though an entire lifetime spent in solitude or pursuit of God or Truth through various meditative or denunciative methods is hardly the path a whole populous could take to instigate global consciousness change at the level I am intimating.

And if it were, then to what purpose, certainly the world will not simply let down its hair and sit beneath a Bodhi tree all its days until death.

Ironically, herein, at death, our last and greatest hope of real understanding (albeit too late) can come to us. Medical records and personal accounts across the globe verify matching 'afterlife' accounts again and again.

Despite the necessity for scientific proof/empiric evidences, no one can now reasonably stand up and say poppycock to such reports coming from reputable medical sources despite unwillingness to entertain the notion due to all such reports being second hand.

Doubt is the very nature of analysis and logic, its limiting bedfellow. Dally into quantum physics even a little bit and it soon becomes apparent that logic is out the window even if reason isn't!

It is on reason that I will attempt to present the initial standpoint for this writing. Fully aware that to uproot and train an entire world separate from daily life will result in global war, it comes to me that through education and media, the ideas I will express can and are useful.

There are already many minds like me in 'service' to humanity, but as yet I have to cross paths with any philosophical mindset that is open enough to go beyond philosophy and theory to fact/experience and proof of standpoint, (likely and I am only speaking generally), because when the parameters of ALL philosophical consideration have been breached, the philosophy itself becomes redundant, as does the philosopher/psychologist etc.

So returning to the standpoint, observer, self (little's'), consciousness construct we call human mind, I shall set out what it is and what it is not.

Try to keep an open mind, most doubts and questions your egoic education raise will be dispelled as we go along.

Remember, belief is not required and what I am presenting is based on its reasonability to be accurate/true, not its structure/expression.

As a short note, I am trained predominantly through 'spiritual' circles of thought with philosophy (western) being a secondary and lacking consideration in my own 'experienced' perception. Remember that goal structures means, and I will introduce goal, after the consciousness outlay section is completed.

Mind: Translated from Greek into Latin as Spirit.

Mind, the workplace of consciousness, a level itself that is divided up into current and sub categories, to which I will add for possible future reference, second sub and also Higher levels.

I am further going to propose for our purposes of understanding new concepts, that sub and current/operative levels are actually the one level, like different rooms on the same floor of a multi-level building. Since we are aware of the nature of sub and operating level and not of second sub and higher, it is easier to bundle them this way rather than to treat them as different sections/levels.

Our operating level is of course the where, what, when and why of consciousness. We experience it as analytical, creative, trainable, and emotional and in many ways it arranges our cognitive associations of thoughts and concepts without much effort.

Yet as babies and children this is not the case.

Repetitive conditioning/training is ongoing until mind reaches a community standard at 'maturity' and from thereon it seems as if no ongoing training is required or available regarding the minds functioning itself, leaving it floating in the vast sea of unknown human potential, likely only to be further trained, similarly to a computer to master tasks and emotions, but not necessarily to continue on in its own inner passage of evolutionary expansion and Self understanding.

Ego, the inner guide/guiding system of consciousness mind is the sole arbitrator of what is and isn't allowed into observer awareness, which is why perception is individual and also why the false notion of relevant truth is so strong.

Needless to say, without a different guide/viewpoint, ego cannot be surmounted or challenged, which is why a point of focus from outside the confines of egoic consciousness is required in order to affect lasting change.

This may seem impossible given that it is seemingly impossible to venture beyond consciousness and return and I am certainly not suggesting anyone need die or experience near death states to bring this about. I am merely saying that an independent non-linear/egoic awareness of self is essential.

Something that cannot be categorized and polluted through individual perception and individual relevance of personal importance based on the setting of egoic goals.

The question of 'What am I?' has befuddled science and philosophy alike for thousands of years, exactly because the level of mind used in analysis is capped by its parameters. It is like a prisoner trying to imagine the colors of the seasons outside his cell. He can only ever 'try to imagine' it. Knowing it depends on experiencing it!

Perception and Knowledge are entirely two different things.

An experience can be registered in the mind as a fact. We accept that it happened because it was experienced. Whether internally or externally, whether understood or not, once something is experienced, it becomes part of our own condition.

It makes and directs our mental composition to varying degrees depending on how relevant we find the experience in relation to our current awareness/understanding of self, and in relation to its usefulness to us dependent on the goals we have or don't have.

Our ego is trained to have us fit in to a particular level or understanding of self, based on external references and stimuli and any experience out of accord with its trained governance of the conscious level is usually (unless correlating data/experiences are supporting) shuffled away to 'unidentified' memory classification, rather than potentially useful classification.

There are many millions of people who have experienced things they don't understand or can't comprehend, whether physically or philosophically, and they 'file' those moments/experiences as 'past references' which is egos' capacity as arbiter of conscious association.

Past, present and future are analyzed and pigeonholed on interlinking references we call thoughts that themselves, although meaningless except by individual perception, build witnesses for reference in our ongoing struggle to keep ourselves safe in the world, to fulfill our goals.

This system of selective judgments based on stimuli and references is exactly the task of the egoic/conscious thought system.

If there is substantial enough challenge to its foundations then a 'snap' or break from the perceivers accepted understanding and management capability processes brought on by conflicting perceptions can occur and we classify that as a mental break down.

Ego consciousness is infallible in its performance of duty, but like a computer, if it is not programmed to be inclusive of 'unknown' elements and if it is not given a structure of continuing self- appraisal and integrating principles, it cannot go beyond its limits within the conscious level.

It will inevitably run back and forth through the corridors of the conscious/sub conscious mind searching for order amidst the chaos of files it has sanctioned as 'awareness stimuli' but which it has not allowed into conscious observer awareness due to lack of relevance at the time of stimulation.

Much like a child who is into matchbox cars will file away unrelated toys into boxes in an attic and then frantically search them out in time of urgent need later in life, but un-remembering of which box they are in.

The ensuing frantic overturning of all boxes and toys etc to satisfy the current need becomes manic as memory relativity (only utilizable in the conscious level) fades and the sight of goal satisfaction/recall seems to slip again from grasp.

The child can be left sitting amidst the turmoil of upturned boxes with no clue as to why it is there in the first place.

Without a separate reference point, it is unfair to say ego is not your friend. It is simply performing the tasks it was assigned through its education.

In light of a new goal, or a separate experience from beyond the conscious level however, it is apparent that unless some mind training is undertaken, the dogmatic activity of ego/judgmental perception may and usually will conflict with the acquisition of goals it is not trained to reach.

If someone is trained only to scale Mt Everest to base camp and then shown the summit later on, it is likely that extra training/skills will be required.

Not always. Individual acumen and tenacity and dogged determination may achieve the goal, but in the case of extreme and non-understandable goals it is rarely the case and likely to end in tragic failure.

It is entirely possible to set a goal without understanding it or without understanding how to attain it, but it is likely unhelpful to have goal(s) that set attainment activity in different directions. So for this purpose then, one goal will be set, Truth.

Truth based on perception is likely to be fallible. Relative truth (as stated) cannot be useful if we are to steer consciousness as a whole to a united understanding of Self, purpose and action.

Philosophy breaks down beyond the premise of relative truth, because like any egoic conceptual association it is limited by its parameters within the level of mind it is based.

So to set a goal internally, but beyond the conscious awareness level would seem perhaps possible, but also just as possibly unobtainable except perhaps by random happenchance. But this is not true. The hope of release from the limits of conscious association comes when the mind reaches a point of paradox.

Many at this point do indeed have breakdowns etc, and just as many retreat from the paradox labeling it too difficult to fathom/reconcile.

But for our purposes the (a) paradox must be exposed, in order that a further stepping off point/exploration point may be gleaned.

This is what I refer to as my standpoint.

In classic eastern philosophy of course the confrontation with paradox is referred to as the void. There are many references to 'crossing' the void, which in my understanding having done this several times, I simply liken to it, as accessing the different levels/paradigms of mind.

Paradox:

When something seems to be so, but cannot possibly be so.

To circumscribe a basic arrangement of concepts through which approaching a paradox is accomplished it is necessary to examine fully the parameters of our ego consciousness/judgmental/dualistic mind a little further.

Duality:

Duality is the concept through which ego mechanizes its decisions, good and bad, right and wrong etc.

It is the sole mechanism for all judgments. It is taught and learned in the mind from the cradle as a total guidance/survival concept.

Time space:

Time/space is the parameter of ego. It cannot go beyond concepts as it seems to exist solely to act as a guide in time/space and maintain the integrity of time/space individual perception for the purpose of undertaking the time/space 'journey' and reaching the time space goal which is ultimately death for all living things. Time/space itself being the transition from beginning to ending, big bang to…

What am I?

"What am I?" is the greatest and 'mostly' unanswered question of all philosophical/theoretical debate and speculation, from Plato's cave to Hawking, the 'God particle' is the current quest of quantum theorists and mechanics the world over…

Religious and ascetic minds have attempted to manifest reasonable conceptual philosophy and principle whereby through faith in the unknown as a kind of personal experiment with the boundaries of death and disease, mental or physical have seen the amazing monitored results of mind over matter in the feats of devout monks and dedicated mentalists the world over.

But even in the case of these results, what is witnessed to is the effect, not the cause. The answer to all causation and therein Truth/origin, can only lie in one place… beyond the paradox.

So it becomes essential at this point to manifest the paradox. I realize I earlier stated I wouldn't go to that end in this writing, but in view of the flow and continuity of the writing which I am myself considering in a good light at this stage I have, in that light or better, in light of the circumstances, changed my mind.

Anyone wishing to remain in the status quo of ignorance/philosophical speculation should likely put aside this writing at this stage, lest the revealing of the paradox causes egoic scrambling and retreat to lesser more 'familiar' conceptuality.

Facing the Paradox is easy if you are accustomed to it. Having a framework of at least theoretical reasonability is about the only comforting thing you can use to usher you beyond it, unless of course you have already experienced stimuli from beyond the conscious/subconscious level of mind.

So now I will put forth a case for supporting theoretical 'netting' that will cradle the efforts to breach consciousness.

It is for me apparent that at this time it will be helpful to refer to some ideas in their 'spiritual' context, as I have found that it is increasingly difficult given the myriad/non-relating concepts of psychology and philosophy, to use more scientific/contemporary terminology.

If I refer to things in a somewhat childlike manner (as I have exampled prior) please try to stay with me and maintain the customary open minded positioning.

To begin with I will utilize 'GOD' as the central idea representing source or origin of all matter/life etc and expand upon the idea of God as we go along.

God:

Formless, Spirit/Mind, All Encompassing, Eternal, Unconditional Love, Source of All that IS

Almost all faiths and religions have a similar if not identical core association for the idea of God.

This begs the question that, if God is Formless and all encompassing, what are the forms and shapes we are and see around us as physical things/bodies etc?

If God is formless and eternal and all encompassing, are we then not part of that?

Yet we appear to ourselves and each other, the observers, as form, flesh and blood.

Either God does not exist and there is no singular source of all life, or our definition of life is wrong.

The offshoot questions are endless of course and one answer only raises more questions. Genesis, Adam and Eve, the biblical 'stories'/analogies of conceptual associations as actions of mind application that train the ego consciousness to crawl from the mire of the evolutionary pit and look squarely at the question/relationship of his own existence... what for, to what end, what purpose?

The conceptual answer I would hold out as a whole activating part of the re-associative effort to 'awaken' man to his true Self is as all-encompassing as the nature of the answer I would give if you asked me how time/space began.

I have the answer, but it must come to you in a way you can use it, or what good would it be, you would file it as just another story that you read in a magazine or wherever this writing may eventuate.

The fact remains, despite reasons for or not, you are reading this now, and are therefore in the bracket/box labeled 'Human egoic consciousness.'

Your death awaits you even as you read on, and yet it doesn't trouble you greatly, there is enormous effort going on in your subconscious to keep the obvious from you, to keep you asleep in your own mind.

But you are now no longer asleep, you are awake in your own dream, I have called you through this writing to simply and reasonably examine the situation in which you find yourself.

Avatar, body, human, your experience of yourself as separate from God, from each other is impossible.

God/Source, IS everything, is Eternal etc.

This 'illusion' - this Maya, of time/space, physical reality is a kind of rescue effort, a vast engineered matrix if you like, in which your mind is a whole and equal part, and like the cogs in a clock, each tick is perfectly engineered to lead you to awakening, everyone you meet, every decision you make, every article you read... every thought in your head.

What you call sickness is merely the manifestation of resistance you have under the auspices of your idea of free will to try and redirect your course differently. But no matter how you redirect or think you redirect it, it is as it is meant to be.

Only time protracts as you attempt to engineer your own destiny. But it is a futile effort; death is your lot unless you answer the question of your Self, unless you redirect your consciousness to a new goal, a new point of focus leading to an alternate conclusion.

'Crossing' the void/confronting the paradox, going beyond the possibilities of your own limited ideas about your own mind

My writing has diverged somewhat at this point and I will likely not review it to ensure continuity or clarity as it is not the conceptual grasp of my statement that I am trying to get to your attention (although that may come fully given training and determination). It is the vibration, the power of my mind reaching out from and through this tiny speck of mortal dust to reach you now that is the purpose of my writing.

I speak from my own experience of the Truth, to that self-same awareness in you. To quote a famous mind of biblical renown, "The kingdom of Heaven (sanity/knowledge) is within you, seek the truth and it shall set you free."

This question "What am I?" has plagued the brightest minds of our times over millennia… until now. It's just a matter of re-education!

Doing nothing is impossible; all things being an action of mind '
doing' whether it be things or no-thing is still an action,
determined of conceptual arbitration.

When Jesus says, 'I need do nothing', it's simply that all things
are included as ONE action of mind already that precludes
necessity of any kind but simple acceptance.

Practiced well, this will and did realign peace as the focal point
of miracle mindedness.

Beyond the self recognition of this as having become automatic,
there IS nothing to do!

Salvation is liberty from all concepts, including this one!

The continual back dipping into observances of associative
behavior is but part and parcel of that Whole realignment.

The joy comes in recognition of automated activity in mind,
bypassing form validation necessity, seeing that nothing ever
happened!

Peace

DREAMER

The script for your experience in salvation has been written already. You cannot get it wrong. God allowed you only so much leeway in your desire to experience this virtual/dream separation experience from him. This is what it means when I said that God set the limit on your descent.

Unless some control over the volume, or better, onslaught of insanity was established, you would not be able to find the moments grace wherein recall to sanity, (even as it is understood from within the experience), can arise in the mind.

Onslaught of insanity is concordant with the individual's desire for the fulfillment of external sensory gratification. The particulars of the onslaught are always individual and chaotic, much as if the pages of a story book were torn out and put back together randomly. The book is still complete but completely unintelligible.

Whilst you can read one page at a time and discern a small amount of sequential data, as soon as you come to the next page, and even though the characters may seem to still be the same, the disjointed script does not allow for the continuity of sequence, and the reader cannot maintain the same flow of understanding as accordant with the previous page.

So the experience of separation plays itself out.

The dreamer appears to themselves as the same person each day in a world which is constantly changing and makes no sense, even though the characters and settings do not change remarkably within the greater experience.

Initially, and generally, the dreamer seems to be cared for by some parent or guardian, who in times of distress offers some comfort until such time as the individual desires to venture into the world as an individual and experience what it perceives as life.

Its first experience will be needs, material and emotional support, in varying description and frequency depending on each individual situation.

Immediately the problems begin, and the dreamer unless schooled by parents who themselves have been enlightened, will have no clue that the problems faced are unnecessary, as is the whole physical experience, itself being simply an illusion of an error.

However, a specific experience will eventuate as a problem, which should begin the dreamer questioning as to the nature of its existence; why this, what for etc . . . ?

Unable to discern any answers the dreamer will then resort to problem solving strategies, offered as solutions by others who have no real clue but can see profit in convincing unwitting others into thinking that they have real solutions.

In the west for example it is a commonly held misbelief that money solves all problems. If you have enough money you can even buy a judge! But the problems themselves are not fixed, only covered, and similar situations will cyclically eventuate over and over again until a *new perspective* is valued.

Situations which get mistakenly labeled problems, can be identified by common themes running through them i.e. jealousy, poverty, anger, hatred, pettiness, neediness etc.

Until the dreamer really begins to take responsibility for these specific situations for a true purpose, (unfaltering unconditional peace of mind), then they will continue to believe themselves victims of situations and circumstances beyond their control, which are actually nothing more than the particulars of their own individual experience of separation from God.

It is only through conscious decision to accept help beyond conceptual understanding that any dreamer can eventually allow their dream to be completely healed and begin to make sense from the perspective offered through the new thought system.

It is literally a leap of faith - a miracle, without which any reference point for a sane perception upon which to make decisions can rest.

There are many courses aimed at helping individuals to overcome anger and stress through meditation and forgiveness etc, yet without some experience of an alternate/true reality that can be ascertained, there is little point to any of it.

What is the purpose for let's say a doctor or therapist to heal a patient only to have them die later, under the false belief that death is the natural lot of all who exist in this world, and that if you're lucky that you might have a belief that will help you overcome the final moment of passing.

I tell you that to experience reality (God) is as simple as wanting to beyond all desire for individual self-gain.

From that point of self-realization, the world and your experience within it will no longer be a staggering list of ups and downs, but will eventually, through perseverance and determination to maintain the state revealed through enlightenment, become a quest or crusade to release from the mind its false belief in the need to define itself through external references and emotional grid points/highs and lows, in its ultimate adventure in the return journey to God/Reality.

The pages of your book will begin to make sense simply by being understood by you as being not understandable, and whilst you will still be free to attempt correlation of the pages, you will become more and more aware that there is no need to do so, and will gradually begin to let the story of the past go, give up attempting to discern the future plot and simply close the book right where you are at and have a good laugh, secure in your self-realized mind that the ending has already occurred and that it did so by you refusing to play the part of the slow old reader and leaving the rest up to God.

And of that we cannot speak!

God is not doing this to you. God has not intent nor judgment. God simply is, and that is all. The nature or will of God, as eternal whole creative mind is of course the extension of itself, or giving.

When you chose to activate the power God gave you in your creation, (free will), you literally excluded yourself from your own awareness of your creator and also *your* creations since, in the Kingdom of Light there is only one will, shared by all as one.

It was and still is, not possible in reality, (the Kingdom) to have a will apart from God, and so you cast yourself, unknowingly into a dream state, this physical realm, that to you seems very real, but to me, as an awakened whole part of you, having experienced the nature of reality in my own enlightenment, is nothing more than a paradoxical comedy of errors to be afforded nothing but laughter.

This 'apparent' reality is unlike your true home in every possible way. Even simple physics will tell you that every action has an equal and opposite reaction, for such this place is, (the apparent effect of one tiny mad idea), and was, given that God's supply to the request made to enact free will contained the ability to fulfill all possibility of potential inherently contained within the request, simply because the law of creation exists here also, (as above so below).

"There is no void/lack in God".

The answer given by God, to your request to terminate this experience of death and reintegrate yourself back into full awareness of creation, (given that all requests {potential} were fulfilled in the one answer God gave), was and at this moment now is for you, the plan of atonement, which you can align yourself with, simply by wanting to.

To most Christians, it is accepted, the resurrection of God's Son.

'The Christ' (of which we are each a whole part), is the fulfillment of the promise of salvation from this ream of horrors, (this world), which we seek.

It is through our own willingness to follow his examples and apply his teachings to our daily lives that we will, through our experiences, come to the attainment of inner peace and acceptance for our salvation from the need to repeat yet another grueling sojourn in time and space.

WHEN we choose to turn our life and will over to God, to be guided by his Holy Spirit within us, is up to us. But we shall deny immeasurable eons, unless our determination, to relinquish free will is not total.

This may seem to the human conscience construct to be an impossible task, given the addictive nature of the human mind in its ability to deceive itself.

Yet, as through all the ages, it is the power of simple honest prayer, that will keep us on track, and give us the proof, which will boost our faith and trust, (so lacking yet so crucial to the nurturing of our frightened and suspicious minds), that we need to overcome our fear, enabling us to finally awaken to our true reality, where fear exists not.

It should be made clear that there is much evidence supporting this statement, and none more relevant than your own enlightenment recognition experience.

For further helpful hints on realizing you're not here and that you do not exist as a body at all, please refer to the invaluable writings of 'A Course in Miracles' and, or, the new testament of the 'Holy Bible'.

I strongly advise you avoid new age publications like a plague, yet should you feel the need to detour into such heights of egoic spiritual fantasy, please feel free.

I am not your teacher, neither are you my pupil. We are one. Friends and brothers, sharing an experience of salvation from separation through the realization, we are One Self.

Yet, for a moment in time, one who temporarily has more, will give to one who temporarily has less, so as to learn that there is no loss in giving, but this only applies to mind training or better realignment of identity, and has no relevance to who we really are as equally and individually, a whole part of Gods' love, the Christ.

Any good teacher knows that his student is only an opportunity to once again perceive the Christ, and is actually bringing him a gift.

Revelation cannot be used as an excuse to use denial inappropriately, or the teacher will himself begin to re-establish false conceptual beliefs and require a miracle to realign himself, which is hardly helpful in establishing a field of trust with the student and which I am asking you to have in me, (Jesus).

Any teacher of mine to whom I (Jesus) have granted revelation has not only earned it but has also earned the constant responsibility by which he met the one condition which initially allowed him his release from fear, that being, that he saw and fully accepted without condition that his interests and another's, were not separate.

Unconditional gratitude is due the student, and all differences in understanding, being only temporal anomalies, ought to be the only thing the teacher is concerned with relieving the student of.

This does not imply that the student will necessarily accept the unconditional gesture of his teachers love for him.

In fact he will likely be initially skeptical and retaliatory. However it is that the teacher must defer the situation to me, (Jesus) for Christ guidance, simply by accepting that the situation is not external to him.

As the teacher teaches, so will his learning increase, and the student likewise will receive the benefit at his own level, this 'own level' concept is necessarily temporary, because whilst equality in reality does not imply homogeneity now, it is the Holy Spirit's task, through the teacher to bring the student to the state of mind whereby he is able to access his own internal guidance and no longer require his external reference teacher.

A teacher trusting in his own ability to perceive the best outcome of any situation has still not learned his one lesson in space time. Until he decides that all situations in space time must be handled through miracle mindedness I (Jesus) cannot give him the instants of time collapse that he is asking for, but does not really want!

Any attempt by the teacher to direct the course of the students curriculum or discern by what criteria the student will give validity and value to the teachers offering, can only be egoic, since the very presence of the student clearly implies a lack of understanding by the teacher, hence the collaborative learning situation the two are involved in.

There is never a moment in which the teacher of God is without a student, and therefore never a moment in which Gods voice cannot be heard, but for lack of willingness and determination.

I heard recently that physics has reached a forefront in its venture to discover the one all-pervading single substance of the universe and I am not surprised to hear that the substance is light...

The final clincher in quantum physics is of course that the physical universe actually shouldn't exist, that matter and antimatter should have cancelled each other out at the big bang.

It's no surprise, to me at least, to hear the universe shouldn't exist, since I have experienced that it doesn't. PARADOX

Infinite patience and understanding for my scientific fellows must come into play here since I had no clue about it until I was shown, and would never have believed it even of Einstein himself, but I can't help finding it funny none the less.

And so, I find myself bound to the single law of the universe (*giving/extending*) and, am then, writing this paper in an attempt not really to convince anyone, for I know only experience can do that, but to make reasonable some ideas for consideration which may hopefully inspire minds in search of answers - to consider an alternative avenue to explore.

The inner frontier...

A funny thing about the mystic (*which I suppose I align myself with for identification purposes only*) and the scientist is that a mystic is completely happy that his discovery cannot be understood and a scientist is completely happy when his discovery can.

For the mystic knows that by the very nature of truth as being non-conceptual thus, non-understandable to the questioning conceptual oriented mind, it is completely irresistible, non-corruptible, and not open to debate, speculation or testing and therefore cannot be limited or defined.
It is only in the realm of time and space where inevitability or potential have any meaning. This therefore denies an all-

encompassing truth by its very nature since a singular reality is not inevitable or potential but a fact. The truth has always been, right here and now, yet remains entirely outside any attempt to discern it with temporal facilities.

It really is simple. I will attempt to put it scientifically if I can, but given that science is a skeptical business by its nature, I do not suppose being offered a solution on a participative basis which cannot be proved to a wide audience, fellowship or contemporary body without their individual participation, will be too acceptable to the scientific community at large at this stage in human consciousness awareness development.

Still, here goes....

LIGHT, the single source of all that is, has ever been and will ever be, is eternal and has no opposite.

That is - completely *all encompassing* . . . nothing else exists!

ALL form is an illusory device produced by the conceptual/objective mind in denial of reality to maintain the grater illusion of separation from reality for the accomplishment of individual goals.

Light is akin to energy, and like any energy it can be accepted, or avoided, but it cannot ever be extinguished; only changed in form . . . kinetic to electric etc.

If we look at light, firstly as the simple idea of illuminate rays visibly extending from stars for example, then we can say that the measurable properties attributed to the extension of these rays are heat, electromagnetic force, ultra violet variations, time and space etc.

All of these are variable and measurable in direct relation to the amount of the extension of light relative to the observer and object.

Then there is another kind of light which also has observable effects, and it is found in a term of reference used in language; Light/Reason.

This philosophical or theoretical use or understanding of the idea of light is observable by its effects on the mind. It is witnessed to through changes in attitudes, just as light rays are observable by their effects also given witness in the mind, through external sensory perception, (*remembering that the senses are nothing but receptors for the mind, used to guide the physical animal about its' environment*).

For it is the mind which decides, either alone or in unison with other minds, how something is or should be and is communicated, but in ALL things the decisions as to how communicable effects are reported to each other comes from the mind.

What can be seen to be measured effects in our external reality can be easily communicated, since we can show in physical format to others, the proof of our observations in data, and allow them to decide for themselves if our conclusions are reasonable, (*if they can comprehend our analysis*), and a basis for continuing further along that line of thought.

Internal observations of our own consciousness are more difficult to offer to others, since reasoning and understanding are entirely limited by individual learning and experiences we have had in our own lives so as to be able to continue to pursue whatever line of thought we find useful or interesting to us for the accomplishment of our goals.

Interpretation plays a large role in the *dis*ability of verbal communication also. This is why we are often confronted with the necessity to change our line of thought, so as to allow for a moment of the en*light*enment of certain concepts to dawn upon our minds individually, and in many cases, as with such constructs as societies; collectively.

Such as with the potential of this document now to alter your individual experience if it is considered to be reasonable enough in relation to the perspective or identity you view yourself from.

Coming to terms with political influences, social reform or natural disasters and loss on a vast scale often deems that entire communities are forced into challenging and changing the way they think and therefore live and act, because of the sudden necessary enlightenment of their minds to new situations into which they must adjust by acceptance of experiences and understanding of events beyond their control, which *seem* to be completely chaotic.

This is obviously a mental process which individually and collectively we are and have been able or unable to go along with since historic recall of conscious awareness.

It is commonly understood what is meant when someone says that they must *make light* of some situation or thing . . . it means that they want to understand, or help others too.

In a perfect world we would only naturally desire to integrate or accept such enlightenment as guides us collectively towards greater union and peace, but here the downfall of human thought lies because the universe and the world upon which we live actually is perfect.

To understand that this is so, a new interpretation or understanding of the purpose of the world must be looked at, which, although I have briefly touched upon it as being a denial device construct of the mind, I will deal with it on greater detail progressively, and perhaps in other papers, since this paper is merely an overview.

Accepted now as a fact, both within half of the emerging quantum scientific community endeavoring to accomplish a conclusion of the riddle of existence through quantum, AND through many beings, author included, who have already accomplished their own conclusions through the mystic or spiritual path of Self-discovery, that the universe as we know it comprised solely of the one singular element . . . light, it could be reasonably put that what is required from this point on, is free and simple access to an experience of the singular nature of this conclusion which would have greater purpose worthwhile pursuing.

After all, what would be the point of having knowledge that couldn't be used to further the advance of more than a handful of academics or ecclesiastics? But, more regards that later.

Given that this all-encompassing singular element is and obviously must be without opposite, it can be reasonably seen that any system of thought which extends itself through society based on the possibility of more than one source of reality/origin must be flawed.

How else could anyone ever hope to understand the origin of anything if it were divided?

There would have to be the possibility of being able to say for example, that the universe flowed or operated in a reasonable manner, and at the same time be able to say that it operated in a non-reasonable manner.

Reason itself tells us that both of these together could never be a final conclusion, since they cancel each other out . . . which is exactly the place quantum physics finds itself at the moment.

A paradox…

If light is the building block or foundation of everything, then it follows that even the very manner or operating principle of the act of thinking must somehow have a connection or resonance to it, based on fundamental understandings or conclusions made in the mind responding directly to environment and identification.

After all, when it is dark we tell ourselves to sleep, and when it is light we awaken. This is a very basic utilization of the mind.

Yet even this can be deliberately challenged and changed according to need and circumstance. Jetlag is an observable effect of such change in the mind of someone travelling through different 'time zones', adjusting to necessity to be able to utilize available light to accomplish goals.

Without a goal or goals, the mind would stagnate, become indifferent, and very likely end up attempting retardation or termination.

So, a summary so far, is that, light exists in the mind, as a term used to describe observable effects of the action of thought, called reason, which effects willful change of purpose relative to utilization of thought to bring adjustments necessary to continue function and allegiance to a goal or goals.

Light also exists in external awareness as energy, which is measurable in effect relative to the observations position.

Now, one step further, and I will put it forth that what is external in awareness as physical form is nothing but the physical representation/symbology of what the conscious and subconscious mind holds.

Furthermore I out that physical external circumstances and situation change is effected **only** as internal mind changes, it is indeed observable, measurable and carries to the individual as well as the mass consciousness. The underlying ability to discern the effects however is determined by one single matter, the goal that is set.

A temporal goal carries with it a temporal result, known by its too often over toned name, death. A non-temporal goal carries its result also, and it is this end to which the common reference of eternity is applied. However the religious ideal and promotion of a realm of light form is obviously only an attempt to continue to define what is by its nature indefinable.

Given that the origin of all that is, (God), is the goal we are entertaining or endeavoring to discover, it must be seen as reasonable then that postulations and philosophies and formats attempting to reach a satisfactory solution could never be brought forth from within a thought system that is ignorant of the goal in the first place.

At this point I will use an example of light speed relative to an observer and object to attempt to make reasonable what can actually only be experienced within the mind.

If we look at the idea of a black hole, (a collapsed star), as something which consumes matter, light and whatever else may have yet to be discovered, then relative to the observer's position, the light surrounding the black hole would necessarily be indicating something which is happening perhaps billions or trillions of light years away.

Therefore, it may very well be that the black hole itself is no longer active or in existence and may have consumed a lot more than was in observance.

It may be growing, shrinking or going through any manner of changes, yet due to the singularly unfortunate short lived life of the form observing it, it would never have become aware of all this, for the light reaching the observer indicating the existence of the black hole, has been traveling at light speed for eons.

To discover whether the black hole was still in existence here and now, it would be necessary to be able to take a measurement actually at the event horizon of the current object, *(hole)*, of observation and sending information back fast enough that the unfortunate life form witnessing the anomaly could discern useful data before that life form returned to dust and light itself.

It is of course actually possible to enter into the event horizon of a black hole, which, given guided trajectory would see you coming out actually any random amount of time before you went in, yet all that would happen is that you would still be in the same situation, except not in the same state of mind or time frame association within your own consciousness.

You would be now in a state such as I find myself. In receipt of all knowledge, able to impart direction and counsel to other black holes, yet in all essence surrounded by procrastinators reflecting your own past fear of the event, until such time as you actually collapsed enough residual time through relinquishment of remaining temporal identity/potential, to begin to get a reflection mirroring the state of mind experienced as reality.

Since the enlightened mind could not, not, now be aware of the impossibility to be separate from everything in its own awareness, those beings and images it since considered to be others and apart from it, without impact on its immediate environment are now by the very nature of the conceptual mind shattering experience, (*which cannot ever be forgotten or denied*), automatically included as what they actually are - reflections and symbols of turmoil illusion, non-existent mirrors, reflecting a false view of reality, but which through a complete understanding, now only reflect the certainty of the denial of the all-encompassing experience, and thus its existence.

This awareness takes many years to come to terms with and residual mental tendencies depicting a dualistic existence must be discarded as quickly as possible to avoid severe mental imbalance, (*an all too common problem pervading inmates of psychological institutions*).

Yet without an all-encompassing modality or discipline, and even to a certain extent, even with one, this process leaves the mind in a minimalist state. It is my own case in point, as well as the case of a few others I've been fortunate enough to locate for advice since my experience(s).

Any mind not in possession of a whole perspective of reality is operating from a position of ignorance at many levels.

The hope of enlightenment and accomplishment of its goals is the only thing keeping it from realizing it does not really exist, and also realizing that the hope/determination it commands literally manifests the continuation of potential situations of denial to perpetuate the dilemma.

Fear really is unfounded since any reasonable mind should be able to see that it cannot successfully hypothesize an outcome based on ignorance.

Yet it remains that if reality were, (*and is*), an all-encompassing fact, without opposite, *singular,* then even in time space that fact must somehow be reflected since it would be an impossibility for anything to exist outside or separate from it, even now!

Therefore it is reasonable to conclude that even this document you are now, (*not really*), reading is a part or a facility within the singularity of your own mind, which you share with every other apparently separate mind, and is then a document or rather an idea that from either the perspective of denial is of no use at all to you, or, from the perspective of an eternally singular mind, is something that you have arranged to be sent to you, by you from your future, for the mutual benefit of all in this juncture of space time, since the transference of consciousness/mind, from the state of separation to the state of singularity is one of union and joining in the non-temporal goal already mentioned.

The actual discovery of this is, at our present rate of technology, a *physical* impossibility. However, given that I've said that the external realm is but a symbolic mirror of our internal one, I am going to go one step further and say that it is possible to travel to the stars and experience that black hole right within each individual mind if anyone should so choose, and the experience of this event referred to as enlightenment is absolutely what going through a black hole is.

If the truth or final conclusion to the riddle of existence is truly what anyone is seeking then why would they be concerned with being the one to find it, in their own way, when it awaits them right now but for the asking. There are no accolades, only individual conclusion. The maturity of this position stems from a selflessness derived by the concern for the welfare of the greater good rather than individual gain.

The clincher to all this is that, it is of course a one way trip, and there is absolutely no way to return, or perhaps better said, that, it is impossible that you will ever be able to return as the same mind again, based on your current limited understanding of who you find yourself to be as a human being in a world in a galaxy etc . . .

And no I am not suggesting that you will die, for that is impossible. Remember that I said that the single substance of the universe is light, energy, and cannot be destroyed. That includes you. I did say however that energy can be transformed!

This is really the beginning of this paper, transformation of energy. So, follow this if you can.

Go back to the big bang. Back before the big bang. Before form and mass. Before time and space, everything that existed would have been light.

Not light as opposed to anything called darkness.

Just light, in an all-encompassing idea of a single direction of always, as one thing . . . which is, (*albeit an impossibility to accurately describe*), the state of Nirvana which enlightened minds experience in spiritual awakening, oneness, everything all at once.

So this state must still exist if it is impossible to destroy it. It may be that we are not aware of it conceptually in our time period, but it must definitely exist in what might be called 'ultimate past' or 'ultimate future', before or after the birth and collapse of the universe of form, since there must have been something before the big bang from which the big bang was able to bang with!

Remember the black hole. It has been described by many prominent physicists as a portal, and such it is. A hole in the universe into which all mass and form, time and space and light is, (and was), sucked, transformed and dispelled into an apparently as yet unknown something!

I will go a step further, having experienced nirvana in my own mind, and declare to this world that the something is, **mind,** One whole all-encompassing self-knowing light.

Yes, I am talking about God, or at least what I call God. Not some judgmental man in the sky or religious ideal, but an all-encompassing mind of light, in a non-dimensional existence of forever, which can be witnessed to as unconditional love.

(Love obviously being a term invented by the language development of man, yet understood enough in this context to be used here as a poor or entirely limited way of describing the resonance or 'feel' of God.)

So if we look at the conceptual mind man uses to negate his way around this little globe in the universe as an interactive map, we can begin to see that it is possible, (*and to me a fact*), that the map encompasses absolutely everything within the known and unknown universe . . . what is within is also without.

The map also contains limits, those parameters by which the map itself becomes useless. Edges. Yet the map itself is also light.

Beyond the edges it seems we cannot go, however I can assure you that this is not so. It is simply that beyond the edges there is no need for a map, simply because there is nowhere to go. You are instantly an integral and indistinguishable part of everything all at once.

But to go beyond the edges of the map (*universe*) it is essential that the map itself, as an entirety of all it contains, also go with you, since your experience of everything all at once would include the map, and for this to happen you must also be willing to take the map and all it represents with you, since the map also is only a part of your mind.

Yet the map, which up to the very edge of it includes you as the witness to the map, must and will be transformed instantaneously as it is drawn into the black hole faster than light can escape, and so deny the ability for observation of process so that the all-encompassing realm into which integration is desired remains singular and unaffected.

So how do you go about this…? Very simply, by accepting total responsibility for the entire universe in your mind! This puts YOU at the centre of the universe from which position it must have exploded or big banged from, and will un-big bang to. Not you a body, (although that is included), but you as mind. YOU, **as an idea.**

As the individual goes about the process of internal reconciliation of all effects witnessed to in time space and all inner thinking relative to time and space, in a cancelling out process, to true up to reality . . .based on the single admission that temporal consciousness is currently separate from and therefore irrelevant to an all-encompassing singular experience, they are actually consciously collapsing the time they would have otherwise used that potential and past mental activity would have necessitated to reach a conclusion linearly. (Which would most likely, at his juncture in consciousness evolution result in demise of physical form commonly known as death).

As the temporal mind is stripped of its time space potential, physical reversal or healing occurs and other faculties unused within the mind begin to take hold and phenomena begins. This however is only a preliminary stage, at which the mind is given a space to acclimatize itself for what is to come.

There is of course a very intense and ongoing psychological element to this, (which I will not delve further into in this paper), which should not be attempted without council, since stripping the mind is considered a danger by the unprepared society and something many beings are institutionalized for, simply because no assistance is available for those who have breached the dimensions of what temporal conceptual associations laughingly call reality.

(Yet it will soon become a necessary adjunct to societies of this world to indeed put into place appropriate policies regarding such mind, for such is the destiny of **all** human consciousness associations, although at this point in time space, it is a reasonably minimal consideration.)

Whilst admittedly this is still just an idea and not yet an all-encompassing experience, it is a beginning point from which the effects of the collapse or disappearance of the universe can indeed be observed, until within your own mind it, (*the universe*), is no more, and you are gone, through the black hole, implosion.

There is indeed a point at which you will realize that you cannot turn back, yet there is no warning or advice that this no return point is looming. Much as if you were to go over Niagara Falls in a barrel, at a certain point the force of the flow of the water will be too strong for you to fight against and you will just have to go with it whether you like it or not.

It is only you who can deny the mind once it has consciously been given freedom to do its own thing, go its own way, but only up to a certain point, at which it will be so obviously reasonable that you have no choice but to allow completion of the event, that to deny its climax will cause internal consternation so acute that you will go mad and likely attempt retardation through deep denial or perhaps even suicide.

Just like a small frightened child being taken to see Santa, as he gets closer in the cue of children, he is prepared by his acceptance that other children seem to escape the ordeal unscathed and rewarded, he is comforted by Santa's helpers, but once at the head of the line he is confronted with the point of no return, at which he knows and must live with the fact that if he chickens out, he will have to go a whole year before he gets another chance.

It all begins however with his decision to want to see Santa and experience it for himself.

A black hole, or your mind's event horizon, is the ultimate Santa. Very simply you will collapse in on yourself and never have been at all. However you also will have no ability to tell others of the discovery since they also go with you being included on your map, and you'll find yourself on the other side of the black hole, before you've gone in it!

But then you will realize that everyone and everything else actually already is what that experience is and you'll see that there's nothing you will be able to do to show proof to anyone simply because there is no proof separate from what everything is. It can only be experienced as one whole, not as data about it.

Even the reading of this document up to this stage alone has offered a certainty of mind which can indeed be denied, but cannot in a reasonable mind be honestly avoided. Much as in the psychological whimsy of asking someone not to think about pink elephants . . . of course they cannot, not think of pink Elephants.

And so the same with reality… The 'you' reading this now obviously cannot avoid the fact that you are a whole part of a singular eternal reality and henceforth by nature cannot be two things at once. One must be false, illusory. The question is which do you want to be true for you, for by that answer will follow all the effects of this decision.

I make no excuses or apologies for this document. Obviously in a singular reality, all things and situations cannot not be other than perfect despite the residual illusory identity's attempts to decide otherwise, born of its own individual fears of confronting its own inevitable black hole.

Everyone must, (and will), make the discovery for themselves, that they do not exist as a form in time/space at all and that they are in fact a whole and equal part of all that is, as light eternal - God.

The paradoxical situation, the physical realm, in which man finds itself, is nothing more than a glitch in the matrix which was swallowed up by a black hole and returned to Oneness in the exact moment it seemed to begin.

Matter and antimatter did cancel each other out, and this very document is part of, (*or more accurately,* ***all of***), that happening.

Linearly, this appears as if it would take trillions of years, yet eternally or 'quantumly' the process happened before its inception; never actually occurring at all.

No amount of reasoning or academic or conceptual conscious activity is able to overcome the paradox, and it is completely futile attempt to do so, only an experience is necessary and only an experience is possible.

And that is that, and beyond that there is no beyond that.

The most anyone can do, (having had that experience of truth), is to write, speak, paint, and sing etc. about truth, in an uncompromising venture to raise awareness of a true direction for a true purpose.

And thus stay true individually to that purpose itself, so as to constantly align the mind in greater awareness with it and as a means to eliminate the value of residual illusory perception (time and space), from the mind, allowing for greater and greater availability of access to the event horizon itself to finally and for all time collapse the distance between cause and effect, observer and observed, so as to eliminate any need to exist in the conscious/physical realm of illusion at all.

That true purpose is to collapse time and space. To tip the scales in favor of returning to the realm of eternity, and escaping the realm of potential, duality, time and space . . . death and rebirth.

You will still be you, but the true you. The you that is one with everything. No more questions about anything - just you as knowledge itself illuminate all-encompassing light . . . One.

The question of which all other questions are a fragment of will have been answered . . . **"What is this?"**

For anyone wanting to undertake the collapse of their mind/universe into their own black hole experience, and bear fleeting witness to the illusory nature of the universe of form/body identity, in the greatest disappearing act of all time, I can only suggest the incomparable mind training of the spiritual masterpiece which is 'A Course in Miracles.'

It has been my sincere pleasure to have never been here to present this at all. Ha Ha Ha . . .

Written through the illuminate mind of David Thomas Phare

I just ran three sets of red lights, without even registering to stop, as if they were green. My mind not registering I ought to stop, at all. This is a little scary. If I didn't know Jesus was in charge of what was happening to me I would surrender my license.

I look at the gauges on my dashboard. What do all these lights and indicators mean? What does this speedometer tell me? I really have to think hard about it. When it comes back to me it doesn't register as anything I can put my finger on specifically, only that it tells me something about the car speed. What exactly, I don't know.

I realize that I am losing my ability to order my thoughts. I seem to be ok with writing at the moment, or am I? What is it I am writing for? For what purpose? What did I sit down to say? Am I writing that or something else? How would I know?

It's not really a drawback but enlightenment has its moments, and they're accumulative.

I've met a woman called Anna. She's quite ready to undergo the whole ordeal of her undoing and already she has had a light experience, which is good. She's also seen the blackness/nothingness/terror, which is good, and is starting to grasp what it is that she has to stay true to in order to maintain some element of sanity as she undergoes her metamorphosis.

I've seen it all before many times. They come in. I listen to their stories a bit to find where they are in their own maturation process and then I tell them something of the big bad facts about God the universe and everything. They are not really big and bad of course. But hardly anyone comes to me actually really wanting to find God. Even if they swear blue in the face they do. I know they don't.

So far only one woman has come to me wanting God directly, she was at the suicide bend in her life, and she found God that day. She had to. She had nothing left.

Most people just want a better life in the world, or want to play conceptual ping-pong with me. I don't do that very well.

Sooner or later in the course of chatting, the big questions, which no religions seem to be able to answer, get asked, and I answer them.

To the mind that is not willing to "Give up the world and follow me", (Jesus, N.T.), those answers are usually confronting, confusing and often scary as shit.

I am used to it. I don't feel the cringe of knowing what is going to happen anymore. I used to, but what the heck. No one ever comes to their own ego death smiling unless they're very, very brave or very, very stupid . . . or have nothing left to lose.

I am getting pretty good at weeding out those who have a chance of getting to the point of no return in this lifetime from those who don't, but it's still entirely up to the individual to actually want to take a journey into hell to recover their soul.

That may sound scary and I should get this right out in the open. There is no actual place of hell. The world of duality is hell enough for anyone who has seen it for what it truly is. But in true spiritual pursuit there is the emotional/physical transformation, which is so much akin to the imagined torment of hell, that hell actually suits as a descriptive analogy pretty well.

I am told that as a guide through hell I am pretty good. I don't know exactly what that means, but I am pleased if I am able to be helpful in any way.

I've been through hell once and recovered my own soul and so I know anyone can do it, but you do have to be prepared to give it everything. It's no merry go round and that's an understatement.

The Course in Miracles teaches each mind to access its own internal teacher/guide . . . the Holy Spirit.

As a realized mind I am an *activated* part of that Spirit in my own awareness twenty-four/seven. Not that I can prove it, and there's no need to thank goodness, but those who come to me who are truly willing to experience something not of their own making usually can and do so.

Not as an idea of *'I want proof of Gods existence'*, but in the collaborative offering of Salvation, in which I am able to be used by Jesus as an instrument of The Love Divine.

Anyone willing to learn to become 'miracle minded' can and must experience one more 'Holy Instants' - the divine light of creation directly.

That's the whole point of the venture, to re-establish communication with God, through the Holy Spirit and set a non-corruptible focal point in the mind through which to direct all subsequent thoughts and actions, in order to purify the mind in preparation for reintegration/awakening, back into the formless Spirit realm, where everyone actually really is already, but *dreams* they are not.

This is good stuff now. Thanks Jesus.

I'm getting a real feeling of being used. It's usually when I get a head of steam up and start talking/typing and then I notice that at some point, Jesus slips into my mind, almost unnoticed and just gently directs my thinking so I don't get too far afield from what I am trying to explain, and so I get the crux out smoothly.

I have a tendency to reach out wide when I am speaking to people, to try to gather them all in from whatever angle they are listening to me from. Jesus helps me do that.

I watch faces and feel the energy/mind of the group/individual. It's actually that I am listening to me in my own mind as I talk, since it's only really me I speak for in the first place, singular perception.

But if I have a loose affinity with what I am expressing then sure enough someone in the group will be looking at me blankly. I can hear when they don't hear. My hearing sounds like an off guitar string in my mind - a note off key.

That doesn't happen much these days, and when it does I can tune the guitar without help, with the out of time mind's appreciate.

There's a lot going on in the resurrection that they need to be dealing with besides just retuning my guitar for me. Other minds are just starting to pick guitars up for the first time.

I have noticed in recent months that I am not as able to teach this stuff as I used to be. Not because I don't remember it, but because I no longer have such a strong personal use for it so much in my own mind, having come into a maturity of re-integrative association with my Self, an uncompromising beingness in a way, which is now pretty much self-maintaining.

I really cannot remember what it is that 'new' minds to spiritual unfoldment will go through. I guess it's like when a women eventually forgets the excruciating pain of childbirth.

But when I see a student of 'The Great Way', (a term I have borrowed from Joel Goldsmith), undergoing their own rigors, when they question me about the ins and outs of it, I do remember, and I get extremely grateful for the place I find myself.

Grateful to be helpful, knowing what it is that they are facing and how valuable any help at all can be, and grateful that I am no longer in that situation myself.

I am straight up and honest with them these days. Not attached to whether that may put them off or not. I know they will have to undergo this in one lifetime or another so it may as well be this one here and now.

What difference could it possibly make, if there's never an appropriate time to die, to live, to be reborn?

I don't know where this is going and I guess it's not important. I am trying to remind myself that if all these musings should ever turn up in a book sometime, it would be nice that they encompassed a wide array of particulars regarding enlightenment and its participative endeavor, and not just my stuff, which I know can tend to get quite tight and pointy.

I read a book by Jed McKenna, his first one, and it was pretty raw and focused on the hard edge facts of what it is and what it isn't. It was spot on too. I recall I liked it and I highly recommend it as a precursor, to anyone considering the real pursuit of truth.

His book(s) didn't cover the physically transformative elements of the endeavor though. Nor did it cover the potentiality for directly accessing the light, which is in everyone's mind. It is these things that seem to me to be important to know about once the journey proper begins.

Without the potential to access the light in your own mind directly, as a 'not' of this world experience, there is no point to unfoldment. You will just be a zombie in a meaningless world waiting for the moment you lay your body down . . . content enough alright, but without communication, cut off from the physical world and cut off from your re-awareness of Heaven.

'A Course in Miracles' is all about this 'light communication' and Jesus actively encourages direct contact with the light in many lessons in the workbook, as well as all throughout the text. 'A universal theology is impossible, but a universal experience is not only possible, but necessary.'

Revelation unites the mind directly with God. Miracles unite minds with each other. It takes enormous devotion and dedication to reach the light. Every mind has the power and ability to do it, since the Holy Spirit is the guide in everyone's mind, simply awaiting the heartfelt sincerity of an invitation. Anyone can experience 'Holy Instants'.

Holy Instants/Miracles are like little postcards from Home. Little glimpses of Heaven, Oneness, and they are fantastic, reinvigorating, void filling, everything like that . . . a total fix all.

Every time one of these light instants occurs the mind is instantly realigned to Heaven, and the reason for and the goal of the curriculum is glimpsed.

My own situation is a little different in that I was shown the whole shebang (Revelation/Enlightenment) instantly and then had to return to the physical continuum to purify my mind of residual egoist thinking, judgment.

Judgment in the usual sense is not good or bad; it's just not anything.

Judgment for your Holiness is ok, and is what you are actively taught to do, in 'A Course in Miracles', in order to see through the Holy Spirit's Vision.

You are asked to re-educate/re-direct your 'self-made' ability to judge, in order to judge **for** your holiness, and I am stepping out on a thin branch to say that whatever judgments you may encounter throughout **these** writing are also in that vein, as an attempt to guide you to an understanding, not to convince you of anything or get you on side regarding the subject of the judgment itself.

It is impossible to conceptualize anything without judgment, and I would not therefore write anything at all, except that I have been guided to, as it may be helpful.

No matter where you think you find yourself in your time/space sojourn, I know that these writings were and are now helpful, even if you don't understand much about what I am talking about at the moment.

Everything is always working for the greater good. Your awakening, the awakening of mankind as a whole, is what the greater good is.

Given that the dream is over, and you are just remembering how that occurred for you as you play your part in your own resurrection process, I can declare the usefulness of these writing with perfect certainty . . . these words you are reading right now were and are now part of your own individual awakening process, right here and now, which is already complete.

Welcome Home

NOW.

If you can admit to your angst and irritation in accepting that you find total commitment to truth through the auspices of the modality or path that has been given to you, especially for you, to facilitate the speedup of your transformation, then you can begin to practice the principles of the modality itself despite reservations to actually convert or release the energetic patterns of thinking that allow you to think that you have any other option at all and simply surrender to what is right in front of your nose.

Don't be fooled into thinking that without the modality you would be okay, because it is the presence of modality of mind healing itself which arouses awareness of the latest resistance in the first place.

It does not really matter what the resistance is towards, since all resistance is only ever directed at Love since form is illusory and actually a deceptive construct to hide Love from awareness in the first place.

Conscious resistance is cleverly stored away, hidden deep within the mind, kept for rainy days, with an arsenal of excuses and alibis' as to why the resistance is justified.

In an altruistic experience of which no other experience exists, resistance cannot not be but a foolish and deliberate attempt to delay the inevitable realization of Self, yet is itself catalyst of the realization.

Inevitably it is completely appropriate in this context since all beings on earth are undergoing radical, mass shifts in the ways they think and see their world.

As with all progressive attunement throughout the race of man, the dinosaurs of old thinking will inevitably die out, to be replaced with those models of thought and subsequent action which best helps man to cope and guide him as a race, onwards towards his inevitable evolutionary/spiritual climax . . . Enlightenment.

This process is easily witnessed to in both the overall plan for man's salvation just as it is easily seen within the disciplinary acceptance of individual transformation, once begun.

It is impossible for the undisciplined mind/man to witness anything but the confusion of his own thinking based on who he defines himself as; a being within a changing world. He must accept fully the particulars of his modality of mind training before he can begin to see the effects of it reflected within his awareness.

This does not mean that he will require a structured curriculum. Religious practice is by its very nature, restrictive of an altruistic experience, and therefore cannot but fail to provide a fully envisioned path whereby all things, situations and events are able to but unconditionally accept as a whole and valid part of God, but it does mean that an untrained mind can accomplish nothing.

Anyone who endeavors to reach beyond the realm of mortality to the realization of their enlightened state must accept guidance both without and within, and be willing to learn the way.

If man insists he does not need help he will always remain in the dark simply because the path of truth is one of communion.

As two or more join in single purpose the light shines forth allowing each a moment of connectedness that continually reinforces the idea of union, and togetherness rather than the idea of separate interests, separate agendas or separate minds.

It is that bodies are only vehicles for experience within the physical realm and cannot join, each having the appearance of solidity and form.

Only at the level of Christ mind can beings truly commune. Much like as when two people in separate cars desire to meet, they must first alight from their motor vehicles before they can embrace.

Man is not really in the body, for man is simply the name given to the species and not any definitive term by which the true nature of the species can be gleaned. What we refer to as man is just the physical/mental structure or projection of the mind pretending it is asleep.

Spirit which is Latin for the Greek word 'mind' is the true nature and force giving rise to the illusion/dream of a man as a form of life, within which the man itself appears to be endowed with motivating elements itself, allowing it to think and report to the mind that it is autonomous and separate from the whole, independent of the One Source of all that is, and unaware of its origin.

Yet Spirit is as it has always been...whole, perfect and unchanged within, and of the entirety of Universal Reality. This is the eternal formlessness of God.

Once man begins to sense the terminal futility of his existence within the form of his mortal experience, then suffering becomes acutely and abruptly insufferable to him in ever increasing strains. He will either seek for termination, through disease and death, which is actually all a cry for help, or he will question his reality and begin to seek for answers.

This latter path of action cannot not lead him to the inevitable discovery that he does not exist. Whilst shocking and disturbing to the untrained mind this discovery is actually a doorway which he will ultimately enter to rediscover his awareness of himself as Spirit, eternal and whole in God.

This discovery will be the cause of unstoppable laughter for many, many days, weeks or perhaps years. From this point his path must be to stay true to the particulars of his enlightenment and deny all the effects of the world and thinking of man as nothing more than hallucinatory and residual punch lines.

He must stay true to the vision/experience he was given in his experience, regardless of whether it was total immersion into God or a vision or epiphany.

He has now gone far beyond his mortal conception of himself and cannot return to it. In fact any attempt to deny the experience will result in a faster death, given that the residual lingering of his distraught ego will utilize the power of the experience and turn it against him in favor of his physical demise so that it may reincarnate with him into yet another life and prolong the inevitable a little more.

Unable to deny his experience and yet unwilling to allow it to integrate into his reality, he will likely slip into complete madness.

Hence the mind must be trained and enforced with the ideas that enlightenment and all of the individual particulars of its devotional ramifications must be accepted and allowed to be the continual and singular overriding consideration of the mind.

INNER PEACE

As above, so below . . . as in heaven, so on earth. There is no separation. Perfection in all things exists without opposite.

Whilst this may seem easy enough to expect and accept of the common day philosophies and beliefs of the nature of the heavenly state, it may sound almost impossible to accept of the realm of form and chaos which is the physical universe surrounding and including the natural world upon which we appear to live.

Not forgetting the madness of the particulars of life, as we seem to experience it as body forms participating in the drama of social interaction, in the world as we know it. Natural 'disaster' and human 'suffering' are part and parcel of the harsh conditioning to which we become accustomed and regularly adjust to in our daily living.

God is love.

With that statement, it is a standard spiritual and quantum scientific foundation that Reality (God) is eternal - a Singular all encompassing state.

This is obviously going to be accordant with a state of complete unity or peace simply because it has no opposite.

Only where an opposite or difference exists can a judgment be made stemming from the falsity of the perception used to determine a location relative to the attitude and location of the one observing.

Where separateness exists an all encompassing singularity is impossible, yet if a totality exists, separation/individuality cannot.

What is everything can't possibly have an opposite. It must be perfectly singular in state . . . and so it actually is here also; in the physical realm/experience.

This statement seems paradoxical in nature, and in a certain sense so it is, given that the idea of two separate states, form and formlessness deny a singular reality by their very existence.

However as each being will eventually come to learn, the physical state not only symbolically represents an inner state of chaos or duality, but also actually cancels itself out through its own paradox and actually does not exist.

Both parts of a paradox cannot be true, although they appear to be, and it is at the psychological wedge point, wherein the confrontation of the paradox jams the mind into a blank. That there is also, unbeknownst to the conscious level of the mind, the potential for the experience beyond which the conscious mind cannot go, yet can experience, a window upon a whole new activity or property of mind....God/formlessness.

This very document, which appears to bear a certain undeniable witness to the existence and reality of the physical universe, cancels itself out by the very nature of its statement, which could only possibly be relevant in a state where doubt is implied.

In a singular reality doubt/potential/time, would be and is, impossible.

Reality/God/light is a perfect state of being....Knowledge.

The dream/illusory/physical sojourn is a perfect state of

chaos…ignorance.

Therefore, if a being/mind, desires to regain Knowledge through transformation of their energetic association they must consciously choose to deny ignorance, (through firstly accepting it is ignorant), and accept the singular premise or attribute of the state of Knowledge, Peace; and begin to use their errant dualistic thinking in such a way so as to allow all decisions and situations in their temporal conceptualization to reflect back to them the effects of that conscious decision, and so give them a reference point from/toward the goal.

All Knowledge is Knowledge of Self, and to realize or experience one's Self, which is of God, one must attain the enlightened state, not just postulate it through conceptual arbitration.

Through transforming the mind, using a modality of mind training, such as 'A Course in Miracles', the individual is constantly inspired and attracted by the correlating effects within its own physical and temporal construct, whilst at the same time repulsed by the nature of its own denial of the singular state.

This is associable to in the physical realm as total inner peace.

The other less desirable way of attaining Enlightenment is traumatically, as a result of perhaps a severe drug episode or depression brought about by a war or similarly futile life situation which is likely to be accompanied by overpowering or strong thoughts of suicide, which brings the individual to its total surrender to God/Self or *the quantum moment* through suffering.

The dawning of the realization of this state within the mind is still only so as to allow the mind itself a true and undeniable reference point by which to take a correct bearing of itself in its ongoing process of integration or re-association back into the awareness or mind level of the formlessness of light.

Yet even this quantum moment cannot dawn unless the mind wills it completely. It is akin to the current of energy powering/animating the conceptual identity, suddenly being reversed and then reversed back again.

Left with the sudden awareness that reversing the current brings intense peace and fulfillment and awareness of unspeakable glory, the being is now left to reprogram itself at its own pace to reintegrate to the true enlightened state.

The conceptual mind must be **willingly** returned to its pre-programmed state through the release/forgiveness of all mental/emotional programming and temporal associations.

In short it must learn to unlearn itself so as to be able to relearn from a different perspective.

Unwillingness stems from resistance, fear, and actually an intentional attack/defense driven mind set.

Peace of mind cannot be stabilized whilst separate premises for both fulfillment and potential are cherished. Separate goals are impossible in the attainment of a singular experience.

Some beings are born into the world and simply realize the meaninglessness of it straight away, and the high rate of youth suicide illustrates this very clearly.

They find themselves in a place of terror, war, disease, struggle, inequality and futility and are seemingly forced to learn political and social ways of such a place of madness, with no apparent hope of being able to make lasting change.

Yet within every human's separated conscious awareness, deeply covered over with senseless goals and mad careers and fantasies, there lies for as long as time lasts, a knowing that there is something else they are here to do.

Unless they are strong willed enough to want to seek an alternative with which to assist their change of consciousness and accordingly that of the mad world, they will likely be swept up in the circus of existence devised by politicians, sociologists and strategists trying to convince us that it is patriotic, moral and right to be a part of the regimes of stupidity that they have devised to try to keep us from questioning deeply into the meaninglessness of life on earth.

Hail as this world's accolades for each one who comes forth, bring forth but scant gloss and mirrors gilded with blood, to hide but the nothingness of its falling joys, and cling then tightly to the hope of a quick and painless death, each has the greatest hope to be rewarded with.

There is no life in this world worth living as but slave to the fearful structured consciousness and all but the few who endeavor to break the chains of egoist bondage will writhe with the worms over and over till the day of realization is seen as blessing not a curse.

It isn't that these beings haven't looked seriously at better ways of thinking and thus being/living. It's just they have been conditioned to look only where no real answers exist . . . within their own thinking.

So change must begin firstly with the way of thinking, from its foundation upwards - a complete reversal or makeover of the mind so as to be able to begin to utilize it in a whole new way and for a whole new purpose.

If there is no purpose to existence within the physical universe other than to deny the nonphysical reality of a singular existence, then what is the point of persisting with temporal asocial at all if the result of doing so is constant struggle, suffering, age, sickness and death over and over again until the energetic association is finally forced into a transformation of its frequency some trillions of years hence in what may be called evolution.

The ability within consciousness and psychological technology exists right now, (albeit in fledging state), for the engineering of programs suitable for social change directing mankind towards an accelerated process of re-integration to formlessness, (its natural state), and escape/awakening, from the physical realm of separation or death.

To begin with it would be necessary to look at an idea of global collaboration even just on the physical plane. Certainly as far as any scale of reference we may use to determine an acceptable concept of perfection in this world, one may perhaps consider that wealth, health and a simple life are good parameters to start from, even just as ideas.

However, this individually exclusive idea of perfection can obviously be seen to fall short as we look beyond our own backyard, to the suffering of those we love or as soon as our own next life drama unfolds.

Peace and happiness never seem to last. At least our ideas of what peace and happiness are, never seem to last, and the understanding of this point is the primary indicator urging self-examination for the purpose of inner change.

For Gods perfection to be realized above and below it is essential then to re-examine exactly what constitutes perfection in the physical realm.

To use a point of reference, an experience of direct union with God, is a good beginning.

Yet to allow the unbroken continuity of perfection, as is experienced in God, to be relevant to us in the physical experience, so as to bring our minds to an understanding and acceptance of the statement that heads this document, (ultimately allowing stability of mind and certainty of meaning through ongoing non temporal experiences), it is necessary to allow and accept new ideas, not of our own making, with regards to seeing perfection and being able to heal erroneous perception in our physical sojourn, so as to realize that perfection, HERE!

To take a mark by which to begin to re-examine the world and universe in which we seem to exist, it is necessary to place the centre of it exactly where it is, with the perceiver . . . YOU!

The acceptance of the idea that you/mind are the 'dreamer/maker' of the physical universe in its entirety is the beginning point for a whole new way to see things. After all, who else is it that makes your decisions, ties your shoes, judges all things, and experiences its own emotions but you?

Until state of being/certainty (God), has dawned upon you, you are still somewhat doubtful as to whether or not you want to even entertain this document as even a part of the total solution to all your pain, suffering and death. And even partial doubt is an entirety of an association of ignorance given the goal and the subject of this paper; *inner peace*.

Take a quick look at the attitude reflected internally given that the goal of the perceiver is now set as Formlessness/Light, which cannot obviously be corrupted since it is beyond comprehension and concept.

And take the next step with responsibility, (but without blame/guilt), as the mark by which your honesty will reveal to you a new aspect of your mind and tell yourself as simply and specifically as you can, what it is that you see. Or, allow yourself to momentarily reflect on a situation that may be causing you discomfort.

To use an egoist example, (since this works within the egoist construct), to attempt to demonstrate the action of mind that can not only clear the blockage of self-identity witnessing to the effects of its own experience, but also bring forth to awareness a holy instant of light communication.

If Fred Smith suddenly turned up on your door step accusing you of being rude, loud and arrogant, you would naturally most likely respond with affront, anger, at the least pity, but hardly likely with gratitude, (and thus continue to foster peace within yourself).

From the point of view of a transforming or awakened mind, gratitude is the only true and worthy response. From the perspective of being the dreamer of the dream, Fred is simply a figure in your own dream, playing a part, like an actor on a stage.

If your peace is threatened or broken by Fred, it is simply because you have forgotten that he is a dream figure, and synonymously and singularly, YOU, offering you either one of two things.

Firstly the opportunity to react lovelessly and defend yourself, and therefore perpetuate and extend the illusion of a 'you' AND a 'Fred' - (duality), and secondly, the opportunity to accept responsibility for the situation in its entirety and release all temptation to react or respond according to prior programming.

Taking the second 'defenseless' option will obviously inevitably produce a moment wherein the Fred character and the you character will stand face to face in silence, the old patterns of retribution and defense are broken, there is a momentary discomfort in the mind as the socially reasonable residual time/opportunity to retaliate or say anything passes, and Fred walks away dumbstruck, or perhaps attempts a second tirade, at which you repeat the procedure . . . conscious defenselessness – self forgiveness.

Obviously the potential to act lovelessly fully integrates so as to eventually eliminate any residual belief that the path of retaliation can solve conflict is gone for good.

This is of course a simplistic base example and the particulars of each incident/interaction will vary wildly according to the degree or level of ignorance/denial the individual operates from.

Adolph Hitler may perhaps be confronted with seemingly more serious effects of his own drama/illusory mind than Gandhi, yet witnessing to any form associations as separate from your own mind is still separation/duality and cannot but foster the illusion of death.

Given acceptance of the fundamental premise that conflict is not a viable option if peace is the goal, I am faced then with the simple admission that something else must happen to facilitate the re-establishment of peace in mind, which will then begin to be reflected in external awareness.

It does no good to shove the thoughts about Fred away into some corner of the mind hoping not to encounter Fred for a considerable enough length of time so as to allow time to heal the wounds.

That never works. No matter how long I don't see Fred for it is certain that the very next time I do see him or hear his name the grievance will re-emerge as a reference for the idea of a Fred in relation to the idea of a 'me', and guilt will follow, denying total peace.

Given that we want to understand, learn and accept that perfection exists 'as above, so below', it must be our perception of the situation which is wrong.

Either that or God is fallible and a separate state to unity or singularity actually exists, in which case God would be cruel indeed and hardly worthy to be associated with as Love. In which case we would all be justified in jumping off cliffs to end the need to persist with any more of our struggle and ongoing miserable lives and would be deemed insane if we couldn't reasonably see the point of suicide!

With the enlightened understanding that we as a singular experiencing ourselves 'separately' really have no choice then, but die and face the rigors of death and rebirth into the physical realm yet again.

Or to pursue trust and faith to its ultimate pinnacle, we will hopefully choose hope.

This then is an outlay of the procedure of thinking useful in facilitating a grounded basis of operating so as to continually participate in moments of healing which by their effects will show you that the process of collapsing the time needed to learn that anger is never justified, works.

Each time the leap of faith to actually apply the thinking is employed, faith will grow, and through continuing experience, which will eventually come from beyond the temporal realm, become certainty.

These outlined steps regarding Fred should not become a method or ritual.

They are intended only as a literary guide to outline and hopefully demonstrate an action of mind which can simply be called forgiveness or accepting Atonement, (which according to this author, is the same action of mind as advocated in 'A Course in Miracles'), which should through application surpass ritual and become automatic, requiring no conscious effort.

Back to Fred…

So, you have identified that you are not at peace. The next step is responsibility. If you are the cause/dreamer of the universe then you are Fred and gave Fred lines to say, and you also chose to react accordingly. TOTAL SINGULAR PERCEPTION!

Accordingly, it is obvious and impossible that you are separate from any part of it, so attempting to deny what Fred has said in any way becomes futile.

If there is an arrogant, rude, loud anything anywhere in the universe, then it must have come from and be **you.** You are the idea of it by your association with it. You are never separate. Fred is only ever an effect of your own thinking.

Big deal, at this stage it's only 'sticks and stones'…but failing to take responsibility, accept singularity, will simply bring another Fred style situation into play again in a more obvious/painful way.

To the untrained mind, the universe of form is completely chaotic yet it actually follows the same premise as God…it only gives.

If you are unwilling to accept what it gives and so thereby move on in your sojourn from ignorance to Knowledge, darkness to Light, the effects of chaos will pile up behind you and give you a sharp shove but you cannot stop mid-stream in a river. You must go with the flow until you reach the sea.

In other words, let go of the scenery of the past stretch of the river, forget about the upcoming bends, and concentrate fully on helping your boating fellows negate the spot of rapids where you are, here and now!

Be present!

In the true humility of accepting responsibility for all aspects of the dream, you are responsible for, both good and bad, sickness and health etc, (since one does not exist without the other).

Given that you remember your goal is singularity, you can begin to take on your own residual effects or 'karma' and have it healed so as the pattern of thought it stems from, separation, can be broken down and dismantled.

It may be humiliating for the ego/separate consciousness to stand there defenselessly and accept what Fred is saying, yet it is re-empowering to you who are spirit, to finally stop being a victim, take responsibility and then take the next step…self-forgiveness. Forgiveness for asking Fred to participate in the dream to show you your own errant thinking in denial of a singular reality in the first place…which must then obviously lead to gratitude for Fred.

Since we all come from, (and actually are now in), a realm of light where the only principle of existence is love, it is hardly likely that Fred, you, Self, likes playing that role for you any more than you like the idea that you have asked him to do so, so as to assist you in your attempted escape from reality referred to as *separation*.

At the core of everyone's being God/unity resides.

It is this fundamental premise which draws us each and every one to ultimately seek peace, and at least see, that peace is preferable to conflict, even if we are confused and believe that conflict is often unavoidable.

Forgiveness employed through this perspective simply sees that our brother Fred is merely carrying out our wishes, and giving us the opportunity to be grateful to him for his loving service, (which is a healing attitude reflecting Self-love). No matter what it may look like!

Anger is never justified. You are doing this to yourself.

Fred has done nothing to us from this perspective, and given that the incident also happened in the past, which is already gone, we can also say that through forgiveness of ourselves for our insanity, (for no one tolerates insanity once it is seen, and suffering, victim hood, separation is insanity), that this is a brand new moment.

What is in our minds now of the past is but memories to also be released and forgotten.

If we offer the entire situation for the greater good for the healing of our mind, then through defenselessness, acceptance, responsibility, willingness to forgive and surrender to an incorruptible single power, (God), we can progress through our physical sojourn and with each encounter, make our relationships pure, as to rid ourselves of the false belief that attack can give us anything we could value at all.

Little by little, day by day, we are led to the green pastures of our mind, to peace and unconditional love seen in actions through the act of forgiving of one's Self.

God, (whatever false concept held of God), must be the goal until it is reached. It must be remembered to be the goal, and discipline of practice, not personality be the foundation of operation.

You can face all things, no matter how humiliating to your ego, if you truly want only love simply because you are not a separate being. You are a part and a whole of a singular moment of always, called God.

You're never alone.

Integrity to premise is the best way to assure ability to track your process of salvation.

Your own inner peace is your guide!!!!!!

Integrity to peace is simple. It requires only the complete forgiveness of all things you think that interfere with it. Releasing one's own over learned ideas of good and bad, should or shouldn't, right and wrong etc... Is the key.

Living one's life without self-judgment, or judgment in general against anything...ANYTHING at all is the whole point of the physical experience.

The miracle is the ONLY tool at man's disposal to aid in this pursuit . . .

It is always a shock to the system when a mind discovers that the analytical way it has been thinking, in order to guide itself through the particulars of what it calls its' life, is completely redundant and unnecessary.

The discovery of the fact that its 'life' is already completely planned out in advance is usually met with enormous resistance, given that the consciousness has suddenly been denied a resemblance of what it would have once thought was its' 'free will'.

The ability to have made or to make mistakes is completely denied, and despite the particulars of each minds experience, which may be intensely unbearable, each mind has, is and will get exactly as its 'script' entails.

From this perspective guilt is impossible.

Each and every person participating in the separation/resurrection 'dream' of Gods' Son, chose to participate and play out the particulars of the universal script, within which, each individual mind has its own part and drama.

Every thought, action, interaction and decision, has already been 'written' prior to incarnation, and the moment of enlightenment has already been set.

Even the decision to return to the formless realm is a part of the program. It is only the questioning mind (ego) which makes it appear as if other choices could have actually been possible at all.

In truth every choice you have, are and will make are already encoded within your chromosomal data package.

You have not been left comfortless.

The particulars of Gods rescue of His Son, Christ, necessarily entailed that illusions of the mind be gently reinterpreted so that the mis-creative error/schism or paradox, which is the physical experience in its entirety, be transformed through energetic conversion back into the formless state from which it sprang.

The whole 'matrix' of the physical realm actually exists only as an elaborate dream within the mind of Christ, of which man the species is but characters, comprised of mutated, condensed light/thought.

The worlds philosophies, religious considerations, scientific advances, mystics, psychologists, seekers and many other identifiable identities are nothing but leading/forefront elements of thought processes manifest within the whole 'matrix' which are maintaining the illusion of free will, whilst actually playing out active and observable criteria of which other consciousness's can follow to higher vibratory frequencies of mind.

The time will and did come when every mind within the 'matrix' began and completed its 'return' procedure to God/Source.

Whilst from the point of view of the questioning mind the details of the grand scheme are literally staggering, in reality there is nothing going on at all.

The finalization of all procedures entailing complete return to formlessness may yet take many, many billions of years in time, yet there is an availability of an offering emerging within the entirety of the script, itself a part of the overall plan for resurrection, that is beginning to be utilized by awakening minds. That is 'the miracle'.

Yet the miracle does nothing more than to restore right mindedness, removing illusion from the mind in ever increasing ways and allowing ever deepening understandings and individual mind's rapid acceleration in their own resurrection process.

The entirety of individual minds participating in time and space, which is the idea of chaos, can be likened to seven billion Rubik's cubes, all trying to work themselves out.

The advent of 'the miracle' simply can be likened to the availability of instructions.

As more and more minds begin to follow instruction the sequences of events enabling more and more minds to find true references of origin will and did increase.

The script is perfect, evolving exactly in accord with the emerging consciousness's ability to comprehend and accept its situation in its entirety.

In a sense there are two scripts. One designed to lead into chaos and one to lead out. Both are actually one and the same, like a ladder which once descended, is then ascended.

Yet the ladder, climber and action are completely illusionary - a dream within a mind pretending it is separate from everything.

Even this document you are now reading is part of your own script. Deny it or accept it, it does not matter. You will do exactly whatever you did do, simply because you have no choice in the matter but to!

It is all perfect, and it is impossible to change a thing. You are but an effect of what never was, believing that you actually exist, and you do not.

Only the eternal creations of light are real. All else is illusion and once over will have never been.

Live fully.

When your resurrection is complete you will be a part of the eternal mind of God and will remember nothing of this. Your chosen dream realm of pain, suffering, sickness, struggle, murder, war, famine, disaster, terror and death will be to you as if it never was . . . Thank God.

Exactly at this point in your script is now the moment when you will or will not decide to become consciously miracle minded through utilizing the auspices of the spiritual masterpiece of 'A Course in Miracles' and speed up your completion process to avoid inevitable lifetimes to come.

Remember, you don't really have a choice. Whatever you decided was exactly part of the script, and everything you have read will or will not be to you exactly whatever it was that played a perfect part in your dream.

No matter your decision, this was, is, and will be a part of your remembering/returning process.

Oh . . . don't believe it?

Take a good look at the cutting edge of quantum physics then, or catch up with the latest discoveries of humanities brightest scientific mind - Stephen Hawking. That ought to add credo to stump your doubting stance.

Regardless what you choose to believe, everywhere you went, and will go will only ever bring you right back to this place - Here and Now . . . . "BE" . . . ha ha ha ha ha ha . . . .

Life on earth, as earth man, is given as a platform wherein I can learn of truth or illusion about myself through witnessing to the results of my own thinking, that show me the choice I have made, to represent my actions, and the resulting emotional response and attachment to, God/love or denial of love.

Being willing to admit ignorance of purpose/insanity, is a safe bet for a start.

But universal insanity, (although appearing prevalent, is not all encompassing given that reason, the modus operandi for this statement, is available simply in a personal and individual willingness to have it be so without condition!

Placing conditions upon reason denies its applicability and leaves witness to its validity in question, in the mind of the perceiver.

But healings potential is always available and in fact inevitable, time being the only consideration.

MY BROTHER LITERALLY IS ME

Which voice I hear in my brother is my own choice, ego or Christ. The answer I give him will be the one I want. This is a singular, altruistic experience.

There is never someone else, someone else's problem, or some other thing. It's always just me.

This is the perspective to reach beyond illusion I must grasp . . .

Thank God for the miracle!

Each encounter, situation or interaction is always and only another chance to perceive the Christ in my brother, for both of us.

He travels the selfsame road as me even if he is unaware of it. He is neither ahead nor behind, but beside me, accompanying me, and without him would I have no way to find the path.

See myself as ahead or behind and still is the path lost to both of us, for no one leads nor follows . . . both share every step, in every instant. My brother represents to me a chance to see a new way to look at and heal an ancient perspective that I have held about myself. He but comes to me to have his chains, with which I have bound him, removed.

As I see him in his role of a body which I gave him, let me remind myself of this: *'I cannot reach my father unless I bring this brother with me, for I cannot claim my Christhood without that I also give it to him.'*

The particulars of the lack of perfection I see in my brother are the hidden things I deny in myself, attempting to keep a little part of retribution available to me should I feel threatened by my brother's love.

It is for this that would have him always be a body in my sight that I can justify my own hidden fears to love myself unconditionally and delay reawakening to my enlightened state.

His fears are but ancient recollections of my own, and the fearful messages I hear of him are but what I have given him to share with me that I may remain in hell and keep him there with me.

He is a projection of mind as am I, yet each of us is the selfsame mind, sharing one journey with one purpose and only one real outcome.

Yet I actually believe each of us is a separate mind, with separate agendas and separate interests, and it is not true . . .

We are one mind, in mind.

No matter what the shifting and changing forms may say to me, it is beyond the form in which salvation lies, in the acceptance in each and every moment of atonement.

There is not someone else ever . . . yet if I am ever upset; it is only because I believe that there is.

I am only ever in God as the love which that is, which is everything that is, whether it be in illusion or not . . . the opposite of life is not death. It is another form of life, and hence, life has no opposite, there is only life; Only God.

The reality of God is formless, yet what I have made of God in my sight alone, within a dream, is a universe of shapes and forms, and it is this which I have done which I would now have the Holy Spirit undo for me.

As a whole and empowered expression of God, what I choose to use my mind for is my own free will. God did not create me as His Son to be a slave to Him.

I can wander off to loneliness and another death, or I can return my mind to him who created it as it was given to me, and be at peace forever.

God is not confused about me, but I can be confused if I deny He is my reality. By denying that, without my perfect brother, I am forever asleep. Lost amidst the illusions of my mind in this, my physical sojourn in the journey of my soul . . . from which I am now training my mind to remember I am already awake and in Heaven, where I never left.

How could I?

God is everything.

Needing a miracle is not really a need. Requesting awareness of what is within you already is really only a request to release attachment to falsity.

Things are changing faster now, appearances of time speeding up, denying more and more the possibility of observational analysis. At a certain point wherein possibility becomes completely mute, the door beyond this world swings wide open!

Peace

One of the quotes I love that comes to mind regarding transformation, spiritual unfoldment, oneness, is by Jiddu Krisnamurti, which says, "If you really knew what enlightenment was, you wouldn't touch it with a ten foot pole."

One of my own teachers, Ted Poppe, also has a similar attitude, he says, "Enlightenment is either for the very, very brave or the very, very stupid."

And of my own understanding, I would add; it's also for those who are without any hope whatsoever, those who are defeated and have had enough; who have absolutely nothing to lose."

I would say to anyone considering the transformation of their mind that they honestly consider these quotes.

Furthermore, if the desire to undergo transformation does not come from genuine heart felt desire to want to be helpful to all mankind, no matter what it takes, I would have no hesitancy in saying to any one that they are completely wasting their time.

The individual must be gratefully willing to surrender their whole life in service to the greater good, not in martyrdom but in anonymous joy without any expectancy of recognition or thanks from anyone but God.

As a teacher of the great way, it is my reward that I have already been rewarded, verified by God. It is not the case that I do not frequently have people offering gratitude to me for my devotion to our Father for them, but it is the case that I surrender all such claim to that gratitude to God, for the healing of Mind as a whole.

True humility recognizes that all praise belongs only to God and all sense of true duty and honor come from serving the whole brotherhood of man without complaint. This should be the only desire of anyone seeking recognition of their liberated/true state.

To be blameworthy, must be the students accepted understanding, not so as to suffer guilt, but so as to experience and offer to this world that guilt in its entirety has no foundation.

God does not judge.

QUESTIONS

There are two distinct types of questions. Ultimately both are meaningless, yet if realization of oneness has not dawned, there is little doubt the aspirant will continue to quest.

These questions will arise from either one of two distinct perspectives; firstly, faced with new ideas, a question may be raised in ignorance, whereby the questioner asks merely to seek flaws in the new ideas, in a time delaying defense strategy, aimed at maintaining its old thought system, for fear of change and lack of self-identity.

Secondly, the question could be asked in humility, coming from a sincere point of truly wanting to integrate the new ideas on offer.

In the first case, it is certain the questioner is fearful, as all unwillingness to release defense is a faithful sign of an egoic premise.

This must be either ignored, which will assure the ignorance to surface again in perhaps some other form, or it must be confronted by pointing out to the questioner (representing the doubt/denial of the teacher) that the defense is futile; only causing delay not unfulfillment.

Unless the defense is dropped, the questioner will not move on.

The teacher, having offered the solution, should have no attachment to a result, lest they serve to endorse and doubly defend the doubt in their own mind given the truth of the matter that what is offered has indeed been heard, and is never lost, merely but awaiting its imminent acceptance.

In the case of the sincere questioner, it may well be that a defense will have to be abandoned, or that a simple acceptance, surrendered to, due to the clarity of the teachers answer will need to occur.

In either case, both are opportunities to enlighten a moment of denial in the teachers mind, and gratitude is due for both.

Lack of gratitude by a teacher is always due to attachment to a result, and failure to remember they are only the messenger.

Inability to answer, and enlighten the moment of doubt, is always and only the failure of the teacher to step back and defer the question to me, (Jesus).

The idea of sickness and the idea of health are the same. One is the opposite end of the other, yet both stem from the belief that you are body.

So long as anyone maintains the desire to be what they are not, duality, (which is what the physical realm of opposites is), it will continue to exist for them and their entire world, since all perception is but the realm of the perceiver alone.

To a mind confused that it is a body, health is only ever possible if it is not sick, so sickness or poverty or equality etc . . . must exist so as to allow their opposites to have validity.

What appears to worldly eyes as perfect health is the natural state of all who deny body identity and realign with and serve only spirit.

The personal testimony of the mind producing this document can declare that due to this alignment process, which has been a continual participation in the auspices of 'A Course in Miracles' for the last 5 years, the physical structure of the body form I am using has not had so much as a sniffle.

To the temporal mind such devotion to 'Self' is entirely unreasonable and it considers the commitment to having unlimited pleasure and release from all suffering an affront to its way of life.

After all, if no one could get sick what would we spend the billions of dollars thrown into healthcare on? If no one could justify their anger what would we do with the defense budget?

If no one could be proved guilty, what would we do with the billions of dollars wasted on the mockery of God humans call their justice system?

Surely no one would be so foolish to suggest that we use our vast wealth to actually help each other for a common purpose . . . God/Love.

Is it just me or does that make sense?

How curious that almost everyone can accept that the body is but a vessel, yet continue to think that it is what they actually are.

To the awakened mind this confusion is impossible. They know that they are not a body yet they accept that the body is not separate from them in their awareness of their physical experience.

They cannot be sick nor can they be healthy. They can but 'Be'.

"I Am"

The total end of the idea of sickness is of course death. The total corruption of the body form and birth the idea of beginning or total health, yet from the moment of birth everyone entering this experience of mortality begins to die.

Some are born into it with shorter fuses than others. Some appear to live into very old age, yet all particulars of existence in temporal association are random and completely chaotic and there is no one who can say in this moment that they will still be around at the end of the day to see the sun set over the horizon.

This sobering thought of course naturally carries with it an obvious imperative for awakening, which is actually the simple acceptance that you are already awake, since God only creates mind Awake!

So actually it is more likely understandable to say that actually everyone is already awake and the process of unfoldment or Awakening is simply the active participation in a process which is already over…much like in an Olympic race…the first over the line, but in actuality the race is already over for all of them.

This does not mean that you need not cross the line. Oh no. That is a mistake many beings fearful of Self-love seem to make early in their unfoldment.

In 'A Course In Miracles' there's a chapter which evokes passionate standing for allegiance, entitled, 'I need do nothing', yet should the consciousness take this single viewpoint as the pivotal axis for its awakening then they are still actually participating in it, but what they are doing is doing nothing. Action and inaction are the same thing.

The accomplishment of anything from within the paradox is actually completely impossible and the paradox is unavoidable.

It is only through divine intervention, a 'miracle' that the 'sleeping' mind, which listens to its ego, can be given a recall of a true reference, (continuing experiences of light communication), point by which to steer itself to fulfillment of purpose and enlightenment recognition.

You are the last one in your own Olympic race and if you can imagine that there is only two of you in the race then it is that the one who crossed first is the only the winner because you are not, but without you they could not have won . . . so both are active participants in an event, which makes the event what it is in its totality as a collaborative venture rather than as an opportunity for separate interests.

Everyone who chooses to experience themselves as a body in the physical/dream realm, starts out in exactly the same place, with exactly the same awareness of being in a world where no one knows who they are, what they are here to do or why they find themselves here. It is as if a great sleep or amnesia has clouded over the whole race of those who laughingly consider themselves the most evolved species on the planet.

That really is funny when you look at it.

Yet the fact is that you are still as you have always been, despite that you swear you cannot remember what it is that you have always been . . . Spirit.

When we are children we usually come into contact with some concepts of God, most likely based on whatever our parents have been able to assimilate into their consciousness's. We all most likely can relate to the memory idea of asking a question to our parents such as, "If God is eternal and He created me, why do I have to die?"

Or, "If Jesus was such a good man and healed everyone and only spoke the truth and they crucified him, then what hope have I to enter heaven?"

And our parents may have very likely simply had no answers for us or fobbed off our questions with telling us not to worry about it. The ego loves to obliterate such questions from the mind simply because it knows they cannot be answered without the mind beginning to awaken from its fog/sleep.

There actually are no answers that will ever truly satisfy the mind, only the experience of Self.

"Seek the Truth and it shall set you Free."

All questioning is a delaying strategy of ego given that the questioner, question and answer all exist within a scenario which is itself untrue in its entirety, and within which, absolutely everything is either assisting in your awakening procedure or hampering it depending on the outlook or purpose you gave it.

Even everything you are now reading is a part of the illusion that is the temporal experience.

Yet, this has had to be written into your script, simply because your world is old and tired now and there is a speedup occurring. Yet even the insertion of this document has been a part of the overall grand plan. And this is the time and place in YOUR story when you read it!

But despite that there are reasonable answers to your questions that can be easily accepted, without some mind training the individual will be too fearful of the awakening experience.

It's a leap of faith that cannot be faked . . . much like if you were to choose to awaken and then one morning found yourself in bed but on the moon. Well it's even more radical than that!

Yet I assure you that you have awakened to your own experience of the fact that you are already Awake, and that this is simply a reminder to celebrate . . .

Shine on Holy Ones . . .

I love you.

THE ONE SON

Once upon a time, long, long, long, long . . . ago, but actually right here and now, before time began, before the big bang, there lived a light.

This Light was everything and everywhere. There was not, (nor has there ever actually been), anywhere this light was not.

The Light was all, and from itself extended as Creation, through all eternity, having no opposite. And the Light knew its own pure Self and knew of its extension of itself in thought, as creation, and there was only one thought, "I Am that I Am".

And the Light called its creation Love, and willed of itself, that Love be its Son and the voice of Love was as laughter.

And the Creator became the Father by his Son, and they were joined in Holiness by the Spirit of Being as One; a Trinity, Yet One.

And the Father so loves his Son, that he gave him free will, which the Son might choose to also create as did the Father, that together they would be co-creators through all eternity.

Well, needless to say, the Son did indeed choose to create, and having all understanding of creation, and knowledge of his own free will, began to think, not of creation, but of itself. And of its Father, he bought forth the question, "What am I?"

And the Father knew not, what his Son asked, for all that was, was One. So the Father answered. "My Son, you quest that which cannot be discovered, for I the Lord, your Father, Creator, All That Is, came into being of myself, having always been, I Am, and you are my Beloved Son in Whom I Am." And the Son fell quiet, and in the quietness, forgot to laugh, and the Son questioned again, this time of its own free will, and a void appeared in creation, and into it was drawn the Son, and the void closed, and the Father was alone.

And of the void, the Creator thought, "My Son sleeps, and must be awakened." And he commanded that it would be so, and he called to the void 'Let there be Light".

Now, within the void however, the Son had changed. No longer light, but mass and form, and movement, swirling, expanding, changing, and the Son forgot and remembered not of its own being, but became list, separating into myriad forms and gasses and elements, constantly changing, constantly evolving, becoming all manner of potential things within itself.

And there amid and within the chaos, waiting patiently to supply the Son's only and as yet unknown, (and unremembered), need was the Light, the Father had commanded, that his son would awaken and not forever sleep.

Unimaginable, was the span of movement and rest the Son endured, constantly changing, evolving, separating of itself, into uncountable planets, stars and galaxies and space. On some planets, the Son became as life forms also, creatures, manifest of all kind.

And of one planet, swirling about one single star, evolved a particular creature, man. And of the species Man, one became, who grew conscious and knew of itself, and as it evolved, so developed its thinking and language and it began to communicate and from its thinking the man questioned 'What am I?'

And as by the Creator's will, the Light commanded appeared to the man as a voice from above, and said unto him. "You are Love, my Son, sole heir to all Creation, and now also Master of all the Universe".

And the Son remembered, and in his remembering became afraid of the thing that had happened to him and he began to weep.

He remembered the terrifying moment the void swallowed him up, and he remembered his Father. The voice spoke to him again and said, "Do not be afraid, look to me always, and I shall be with you my Son and you shall not want, nor shall you weep, and the time shall come when unto your people I shall myself descend upon one who will lead you out of this place and restore you unto me.

Until that time take comfort in me and have peace in your heart, and share it with all. I will that you be happy and in this manner so you shall be, and as you are the first to remember, I shall call you Adam."

And Adam abided with the Light for the longest time, and the Light was in him and with him, and he stayed with the Light all through that land, teaching others of the Light, and of the way of sharing that the Light had told him of.

And as he taught them, the Light shone from him into them and in this manner they also were made aware of the Light. Many however could not understand Adam for they slept ever so deeply and they were frightened by him, and drove him away from them with beatings and screaming.

Yet Adam was ceaseless in his virtue, sleeping not, but remembering his Father, and he grew ever stronger in his sharing, until one day there were no more with whom to share, and Adam asked of the sky above him, "Father, I am finished in this task, none remain but those who are not yet born, and they cannot hear of the sharing, but given the passing of time I shall indeed go even to them and tell them of it should you will it of me".

And the Light commanded, spoke and said to him "Go Adam and rest until that time, into the valley beyond. There have I provided for you. There will you walk no further, but will lay down with one like yourself, a woman, who I have called Eve, for she like you is awake and has consciousness, and like you I have given her the word of me, and now she awaits you even unto this very day."

Well as you imagine Adam was pleased to at last rest in his journeying, and he did go to the valley. He followed the flow of a mighty river for three days. With each step he took the river became narrower, and at last became a stream, and at the head of the stream, Adam found the water bubbled up as life, from beneath the ground.

He stopped and fell to his knees in amazement, for there in that place appeared to him all manner of edible tree, and every kind of creature, those of which he had seen in his vast journeying and those he had not.

And among all the wonder of this place, there stood Eve. She was to him a vision of the like of which he had never before beheld, radiant as of gold, pure as snow.

And to her, Adam was the same. And for uncountable days, they lived in that place, and had many children. And the children had children also, and they all abided with the light and were happy.

But Adam knew in himself that soon he must go from that place, and journey once again, to share with those now grown, who before could not hear.
But when he told Eve of his promise to do so, she became upset, recalling the past to her mind, of the time before he had come when she knew not of his beauty. And she became sad, and cried, and within herself she scolded the light for his journey, and anger was born.

And from this birth Eve resolved to do all she could to keep Adam from leaving. And so she told Adam lies, saying that the light had spoken to her and had told her to tell Adam not to go, and that the Light was so pleased with him, that another had been called upon to fulfill the task.

Adam became confused, as to why the Light had not told him directly of these things, but he knew that Eve was like him, and so he resolved to abide in her message, and to put his questions to her aside. For within himself, he also was glad another had been chosen to replace him and that he need not go.

But somewhere deeper still within him, the question remained, though he chose to avoid it, to stay with his Eve. But there it was, ever present, eating away at him, and within himself he knew something was amiss, and he was torn between trust of his beloved Eve, and the wondering of whether he should raise the question to the light.

For he knew also that the Light had not spoken to him for a long time, and he feared the Light knew of his question and was waiting to answer it, and that the answer might see him once more journeying, and leaving Eve, and this Adam had decided he could not do.

And so, finally Adam could take no more of his inner turmoil, and he cried out within himself to the question 'Go away from me, and leave me in peace, for I am happy with my lot and that is the will of my Father.'
And the question was gone again, and Adam was at peace again, but where the question had been, now was a void within him, and Adam felt guilt.

Adam wept for a long, long time, and he knew not why he wept, but he knew that there once was a time he did know why. But he could not find it in him, and in his forgetting he returned to Eve, but she was not the same, she had lost her radiant glow and was becoming an old one.

And Eve, looking upon Adam, also saw the elder and she sank in her heart and she held him to her, and together they wept, and together they became asleep.

And it came to pass, that because of these things, that all their children left that place, and went about in that land forming tribes.

And it came to pass because of these things, the Light was forgot, but the Light would keep its promise still, and would indeed in day descend upon one itself, and lead its Son home.

And that would be our Lord, and Savior, Jesus Christ.

AMEN

The path to knowledge is a burning inside.

If it is not the thing that drives you mad to know of, there's no point pursuing it.

Knowledge is a total state.

There is no room for it in a mind that does not clear away the junk of conception to allow knowledge total space.

No one but a madman tries to fit size 12 shoes into a size 6 box.

No one puts new wine into old skins!

There is no separate disease apart from what you are. You are what you think.

Saying that you have cancer or tuberculosis or any other condition is not the disease called death, which is itself a condition made manifest by the idea of separation.

Any mind associating itself with its identity as a body, is what the idea of death is. The grounding factor of all temporal/body association is that bodies die!

If the disease is real then healing is impossible. Yet it is precisely because it is not real, since it is causeless, that it can be healed instantly.

Because you are not your body, you are spirit (mind), this healing would necessarily entail that loyalty to the premise of mind that finds disease acceptable (ego) be ended.

This will only be accomplished when it is seen by the mind that the foundation for its idea of death, (namely that it is a body, separate of other bodies), is indeed an impossibility.

Any human consciousness association believing it is in any way separate from the whole is bound to suffer and die over and over because there can be nothing outside what is everything.

Furthermore, any mind that has not had its own enlightenment recognition experience, still actually believes in this. It has not yet accepted atonement for itself, despite that it may swear black and blue that it does not believe in a power outside itself.

This experience will indeed come to every mind in time, but it is time itself that each mind is urged to become accountable for in this regard, given that it is only the sleeping/dreaming mind that believes in the need for time.

This is why the importance of becoming miracle minded quickly is necessarily important, not only so as to enable the mind to be of service to other minds, but so as to minimize or abate the ability of the ego to re-establish its perspectives once it realizes the threat of mind training/spiritual alignment.

Any awake, (freed), mind participating in its own resurrecting association, not only realizes that time does not exist, but also literally cannot conceive of a purpose for such a concept, given that the availability of an action of mind enabling them to be everywhere at once, is here and now.

To the awakened mind, fluent with its single purpose, it is only its continual truing up to this, in denial of its own past denial that it is concerned with.

Thus the 'here and now' literally becomes its perspective in all situations, even to the point of no longer needing even this thinking as a reference, as it slips ever increasingly 'heavenward' through its transformation, across the threshold of conscious thought into the realm of instantaneous abstraction . . . .
Beingness !!!

Believing in two powers or two sources of reality from which it is possible to flippantly choose allegiance to according to perceived needs, must and will and does cause ill effects, simply because the mind itself, despite constant conscious/sub conscious observations, (ego) is constantly striving to attain/align with its highest point of reference, its origin or Self, and cannot hold two thought systems simultaneously since reality is one . . . God/Love.

The conscious nature of the human being can and does attempt to deny even this, even though it holds that the highest integrity of its own awareness is always a worthy and just thing to stay true to.

This is seen as simple fact by simply listening to what a mind in denial says of itself. It becomes apparent to an awake or 'awakening' mind that mind in denial, even its own mind, contradicts itself continually yet is unaware of it!

This is why it can think one way yet act another. As the awakening mind becomes more vigilant of its thinking, such splits inevitably become less and less tolerable. And it will seek out higher and higher models of integrity by which to take bearing.

'A Course in Miracles' reasonably offers the most obvious model of integrity of mind available on the planet, since it is comes from that part of mind which has already resurrected . . . Jesus.

However, until enlightenment, at any tick of the clock human mind can be thrust into despair by its own intrapersonal thinking or its intrapersonal thinking about others, that it thinks it is effected by.

Because of this it can radically shift from an integrity based on its concepts towards peace and love, directly into one of blame and revenge which is of course insanity given that there cannot possibly be two 'everything's.'

It is the total commitment to a single premise, TRUTH, which is the initial stumbling block to every human consciousness in this world.

Denying that this is reasonable, the split mind ultimately collapses, unable to accomplish its chaotic allegiance to its shifting and constantly assailable beliefs, and the body eventually succumbs to the tirade of conflicting impulses and shuts down (dies) again, drained of the availability of free flowing healthy energetic pulses giving it power to enable sustained kinetic viability long enough so as to complete its sojourn/purpose in time and space, which is simply the acceptance of atonement.

Just as in a computer that crashes if it receives too many conflicting commands, so the physical projection of the mind (the body) crashes and must be rebooted (reincarnated). Yet if the program is not repaired then the system will ultimately crash again, and again.

It is only when the mind realizes its own insanity that it comes to realize it cannot commit to two separate directions at once, and must choose to then commit to one or the other.

Whilst a commitment to light/reason, is obviously preferable to a mind still able to see reason, it is not always so obvious to a 'blind' mind, in denial, and it can legitimately choose the path of darkness/insanity.

It is not that this path cannot achieve the desired goal of unity consciousness; even this is possible if the mind does it totally.

Yet it is that the particulars of this choice cannot not become so chaotic and confusing to the follower, that they will likely even forget their allegiance and simply lose all ability to comprehend themselves whatsoever.

They then become no use to themselves or any other mind, other than as a point of reference which seen rightly is actually totally useful. However, most human minds fear insanity almost as much as they do self-love and will go out of their way to avoid allowing such an extreme model into awareness.

Many minds may have many such disastrous life situations such as war, famine, rape, abuse etc, which may force them into submission to God for help, and so bring about their enlightenment through 'crisis', yet they will likely end up institutionalized or medicated simply because there may have been no availability of or willingness to undergo mind training participation, to stabilize the completely ego shattering experience.

Many asylums are filled with minds that have been radically changed by enlightenment and or phenomenal associated happenings, but which have not accepted accompanying programming.

Enlightenment is not a blueprinted or casual occurrence. It requires, unless complete extraction by source occurs, that on both sides of the occurrence that the mind is willing to accept direction.

It is important to remember that each mind *chose* to experience itself in the physical realm, albeit an effect of a single mis-creative thought and so must by its own free will, consciously choose, through its own participation in its resurrection process, via love and forgiveness, to return to Eternity.

When the mind sees joyously that ALL effects of its decision to remain separate are healed simultaneously with its decision to return to sanity, then it quickly includes what it would have once regarded as symptoms of sickness, into its new awareness by accepting that they are actually effects of healing occurring.

This brings instant peace to the mind, and despite that there will obviously be some amount of faith required during the initial transition period, it is that eventually, depending on the ongoing willingness of the individual to stay vigilant for the new way of thinking, that sickness will become impossible.

After perhaps a few years, or less, (or more), the individual will no doubt realize that vitamins, health care, nutrition etc, are a thing of the past, since the body, an effect of the mind, responds in perfect health once the mind is freed of its destructive thinking.

This is an impossible tenet to any mind still fixed in the belief that it has needs it must meet, goals it must reach or retribution it must exact.

No one can experience or even truly believe it unless they actually walk and talk the path of singularity.

Yet to the mind in pursuit of enlightenment, it is an obvious effect of the reversal of its death sequence in its acceptance of life as eternal…

Which is what everything is!

Love

There is no way out. There is no out to get - no here at all. This does not exist at all and there is no me who is typing this document. I do not exit.

That which I am has no concept at all and merely is; existing now, only as a memory in my mind.

Yet my mind is not my mind - the 'me' of the mind is not real. Only 'I Am' real and I am not this typing this. I am insane - a memory within my own and I have realized I don't exist.

That I do not really exist at all as anything more than an idea fixated on itself, dreaming a dream of being nothing with the ability to experience being nothing.

I do not exist. That which does exist is eternal. I have another I, an eternal I, an I which knows not of me which does not exist, writing this document which doesn't exist.

Nothing exists. I am dreaming a dream of me being a thing writing this document which does not exist. I am in a kind of coma - a sleep. Yet I am awake to it and am awake within my own coma.

No one can help me waken from the coma. Everyone else is here as a dream image with me in my own coma dream, billions of images which do not exist.

Nothing Exists. I am not here in this world writing this document. I am eternal light in a coma fixated on a memory of a dream unable to awaken yet awake.

Nothing is real here. Nothing is real at all, not even me writing this document. Only when I remember that it is a coma do I remember that I am awake in a dream, I am waiting for someone to wake me up.
I don't know when that will be but I am awake inside my own mind already. I am awake - there is no world.

I no longer sleep. I am awake, awake, awake!

I am not asleep. I have awoken from the amnesia of my coma dream and have realized the universe is not real. It is all a dream. Am I mad?

Am I just awake? I cannot tell anyone. Everyone is just an image in my dream, but I have met others who know this is a dream.

Others of me - aspects of my mind, reflections and not true also but no less not true than me writing this which does not exist.

Yet there is nothing to say to them that is true and they know it, because I know it. Yet perhaps others are out there who will believe it, who have seen what I have seen. They have seen.

Perhaps there are other ones I will find who will be willing to go through complete insanity armed only with laughter and me, who will find the truth. I hope so. I do not wish to be the only one awake, if someone shares this with me the torture of it ends. Jesus shares it with me…Thank you Jesus!

He waits for us all. He waits for and with me. I think I am ready.

I have seen it; HIM… But I do not know if I am ready.

Why am I still awake in a dream? Why have I not been extracted? But I have been. I have seen that I have. I just don't know when.

Send them to me Jesus. This coma is an awful place to live without meaning, and they are my meaning now, my only reason to still remain here.
To help them reach the truth that the great reversal can occur quickly. The scales of this coma will tip because they did. I have seen it, seen me, awake.

Send them to me to show me my denial. Thrust me into the belly of this madness. Send me the reaper. I am afraid but I have nothing to fear.

I which am afraid do not exist. Bare your fangs at me clearly harbinger of doom. You cannot hide in here forever.

I am willing to look you in the eye and laugh. Take your bony hand. Tear the page of sacrifice from the book and damnation and shove my blood red signature down you green toothed face and laugh.

Though I have seen it done, I have to do it. I am in time, this coma awake, before I awoke proper. I HAVE SEEN THE VISION.

I have the vision. I cannot let it go. It is my mind now. I am that vision here. I am the one. Not awake in the dream but awake from the dream.

I know the truth. There is no death. I do not exist as this thing writing this document. I am eternal.

I am not the only one awake, but I am the only one as mind as a whole and equal part of a mind asleep, a single self we all share as figures within it, thoughts within a mind asleep/a coma.

Yet all is One . . . One Self in sleep. One mind, dreaming of itself as many, yet nothing exists. Call me mad, and as this thing typing, I am indeed, for the dream is madness, and I have accepted it and am no longer mad, but awake, among the mad, who sleep and have not seen the truth.
Yet they too are awake for I am awake, they are not man but am I, they are me, not me typing this but me, as eternal mind, awake, fixated on a dream long over yet still to end.

I have been sent to end it. There are others like me who are me; Me awake in the dream helping to end it; to tip the scales. It will end because it did, now.

David Phare, the dreamer of the dream, figure utilized by the eternal mind . . .

AWAKE

THERE IS NOTHING OUTSIDE ME

Everyone and everything that comes individually into my external or for that matter internal awareness during any given moment is only ever my mind interacting with me, in an introverted manner in denial of God/the whole.

Only in the state of beingness is love extended/created. This state is what heaven on earth is, and it is by its very nature nonjudgmental and all inclusive.

It is aware of itself and all other aspects of its awareness as only its self, whether in form or not.

In a state of beingness there is no thing coming into my awareness that disturbs or changes my awareness in relation to other things or thoughts, each is accepted as wholly beneficent and perfect.

Each moment I am aligned or in a state of beingness the demands of the ego reality disappear entirely and only peace is experienced.

There is nothing to think about or plan or arrange and any attempt to do so instantly takes me out of the state, yet whilst in the state, there is nothing that may be asked of me that I cannot do and still remain in the state of beingness.

Only self-determined will removes me from the state. Yet even this once realized can be incorporated or released and the state be re-assumed instantly.

The state of beingness is a singular emotional state in which term 'I am' best describes the mindset. Yet to attain a constancy of ability to attune to and stay attuned to this state, sincere and determined mind training must be accepted and practiced. By staying aware of the altruistic nature of Mind/God, I can simply say yes to everything knowing that it can only ever be God who asks.

Despite that my ego will attempt to dissuade me in favor of safer options than follow guidance that will inevitably lead me to deeper and deeper levels of fear until total responsibility for the seething hatred that lies hidden within is exposed, confronted and healed through grace.

There is never a moment I need disagree with anyone. For it is only me who gives the words I hear meaning or the scenes I see through my body's eyes validity, whilst all are illusion in their entirety and only symbolic representation of my state of mind.

That is . . . the reflection of what I want to be my reality, a world of love or one of dualistic interpretation founded on the idea that I am a body and will die.

Each person is only ever coming to me with the message I have asked them to give me, playing perfectly the role I have given them to play for me in, firstly, my dream of death, and then secondly with forgiveness as my stanchion . . . my dream of salvation.

Ultimately my dream of salvation will, is and did totally stabilize through my application of the miracle principles of 'A Course in

Miracles', and I will and did, (given that the dream is over), attain a singular uninterrupted state of 'Beingness.'

I resurrected because Jesus did and in an altruistic experience, I am not separate from that mind.

All that any consciousness association need do who requires salvation is align themselves with the frequency of that Christ mind and be willing to not return to the old ways of thinking. God is a universal force that has no opposite.

To align with illusion is not to escape God, but merely to bury ones head in the sand in denial of the heard of wild elephants stampeding towards them.

Elephants don't play your games, and neither does God.

God is!

Think of heaven (creation) as a giant unending kindergarten, filled with the purest innocence of love children possible, watched over lovingly by God. You belong (and in truth, are) in this nursery even now. Yet you sleep in unawareness, unable to enter the realization of this innocence due to the potential you insist on retaining in your mind of worldly/separative possibility.

Thoughts make or create the reality of which you are aware and yours are hell bent on attempting to manipulate the physical, whilst your reality exists in formlessness.

You are akin to a mass murdering psychopathic pedophile in your semi-unawareness of yourself, in your deep sub conscious, and there is no way you will be allowed to roam eternity with a sullied mind like that.

Everyone is vaguely aware of their deep hatred and anger, and aware that it is not so much even this that provokes them. It is the question of why it exists, what it is meant to cover in the first place that drives the mind into attempting to control its reality as it finds it.

The realization of God, that would end the individuals dreaming forever, is hidden deep beneath this psychotic chaos of mind, deep out of conceptual reach, shielded for all time lest the truth come to dawn and set the dreamer free. This is the ego's purpose that YOU gave it. It is not God's purpose.

The body is the symbol of the ego, and whether enlightened or not, its existence is only ever witness to denial.

The purpose of the body however stands quite apart from its symbolic identity, and has the power to enslave it to servitude in death or to set it aside through service to life.
Of itself a body/vehicle has no purpose. It is the mind that gives the vehicle meaning and decides upon which goal the body will serve, each with diametrically opposed results.

Holy purpose sees the body as, servant willing, to truth, using each encounter the body has as means to relinquish physical dependence/validation and regain God dependence.

Utilizing a final set of concepts, principles set forth in holy pursuit; the mind eventually has success in liberating itself from egoistic premise, and begins the purification process that will ultimately see it free again, as it has always truly been.

The time this takes is individual, dependent on how fed up with the thinking of the world the aspirant is.

If the ego could attain liberation it would smash reality and destroy all innocence, but it is simply because the ego is nothing but illusion, that all it can seem to do is but keep the mind asleep in dreaming of separation from God, of which of one thing only it is sure, it has a use by date.

Eventfully all minds as whole mind, will awaken, simply because time space has both beginning and end, and because Gods will is functional from within the dream, as outside of it.

The goal is always to purify the mind so as to allow it to awaken/return awareness as divine child, un-conflicting with reality, pure as it was created by God.

Whilst the task seems vast, the grail far off, it is the divine within that does the work, not the mind that denies it. The old saying that, the price of peace is eternal vigilance is as true now as ever it was.

This is why the allowance of reintegration into formlessness is overseen by holy ones, not you; and when enlightenment dawns upon you, you will be glad and grateful it is so.

If it was up to you, you would stuff it up royally.

Imagine a small child being given the entry codes for a nuclear device . . . need I say more.

Actually I will.

That analogy is not so far afield from how it is, given that the void you will cross in consciousness prior to enlightenment is what the event horizon of a black hole is in form.

It's bigger than nuclear!

This is a story to direct the reader along a journey. It is the story of the enlightenment of my mind.

The story itself merely sets the course, you have already decided upon the destination.

When I say *my* mind, I do so with the understanding that minds are actually joined at the higher level, and so at some point in time, perhaps today or tomorrow but only ever in the now, it will inevitably be, and so is, *your* story too.

I write it for me, for you and for anyone who is drawn or inspired to read it. It is a step along a journey, perhaps your first consciously directed step, perhaps not. It doesn't matter.

There is no need to write it or not write it, and when you have read it, forget it, its purpose will have been fulfilled.

Know that in reading this, you are participating in a happening, something that will affect the entire universe, serving the greater good.

Whether you believe this or not, does not matter. Since there is but one mind ever doing anything anyway, spiritual/religious consideration or those of belief are irrelevant, no matter what fragment of mind is reading this, it's always me, one mind reading, one mind waking up, the awakening of mind cannot be stopped, but individually you can choose to delay.

This decision however would only constitute more pointless suffering. All is one.

To cleanly understand the total premise of awakening, it is necessary to understand and set the goal, and be about whatever means are relevant to reach it.

Understand that, losing sight of the goal is what the ego desires the mind to do. It will attempt to persuade the mind with all manner of glorious or depraved offering as it thinks will best suit your purpose.

Even now, there are other things attracting you away from reading this, a bird singing, a child calling out, a thought of better things to do.

Something will always be tempting you to cease any activity aimed at higher vibration of consciousness and the true greater good.

Not the greater good of Queen and country, humanitarian aid or compassionate delegations.

That which best serves the greatest good of all, is your spiritual awakening.

How it serves is beyond all understanding and any need to know. Yet when you awaken everything will be clear to you as never before. It will be as if you have just been brought to life, aware of all things, all minds and free at last from all fear and death.

The more that awakens, the more that awaken!

Given that enlightenment of mind is attained through reaching a total state of inner peace, (or through a total state of chaos which I do not recommend due to the ego's tempts on this path to induce suicide), then purpose of all activity and thought must be to enhance the minds ability to stay true to the goal of peace through the practical application of spiritual concepts and disciplines.

Yet liberation from even these premises is within range of the goal also.

An untrained/undisciplined mind can accomplish nothing. No matter which path you choose to take, dedication to the goal must be total.

I have met many who tell me that they are on their own path, and that's great, but the path to unity has no way, it is a shared path upon which we all walk together, side by side.

The idea of an own path is simply looking for the path. Not this path or that path, just *the* path. There are of course many different disciplines to mastering the art of finding and staying on the path, yet there is but one path, one goal and one traveler.

Never underestimate the power of mind in denial (ego; it draws on the power of your errant/weakened sense of will to weave its demented illusions to keep you in the meaningless hell of physical reincarnation lifetime after lifetime.

It does not want you to remember the unspeakable beauty and love of the eternal realm, the creator . . . God.

Its goal is to keep you prisoner, in the physical realm as long as possible. This is a goal you assigned it; this is the secret you have tried to hide from yourself since time began . . .

"You are doing this to yourself."

To free yourself from reincarnation you must learn to call upon the power of the universe to sustain you as you turn towards the offering of eternal life.

When the goal is reached you will no longer need sustenance; you will have knowledge. You will know and be that which you truly are . . . Eternal.

Without that you become completely dependent on God to lead you toward Him, you will fail.

Yet no one can really fail who truly seeks to reach God, yet time can imprison as well as release, and so it is time the student must learn to master and use to advantage.

Learning how to collapse time is the main focus of spiritual learning, praying for longevity, as a means to do this is not the proper use of time and results in a split purpose of the use of the mind, which is attempting to reach a unity purpose.

Many old spiritual practices are now very outdated, and apart from sentimental or traditional value serve but to engage the mind in a subtly cloaked practice, which actually leads the student down a slow and winding course, often never catching sight of the goal.

Those entrenched in traditions of religious practices or other spiritual considerations will likely defend them, yet those who are free know that there is only one true and final use for any defense or tradition . . . to lay it down.

There is no point attempting to transcend the world/worldly mind, nor is there furthermore any point to endless meditations aimed at better reincarnations.

There is a whole new way of releasing egoist premise which can be practiced temporarily, which simultaneously teaches the ego mind to heal itself, whilst just being about daily activities making practice simultaneously redundant.

Many old traditions are by their nature fixed in time and space and deny altogether the very goal they are attempting to offer.

Freedom from all form/practice/prayer…freedom from concepts is the goal of all who seek true liberation.

Discipline thus becomes eventually, unnecessary, and as the mind becomes more and more naturally abstract, it loses the ability to discern the need for healing, ergo, spirituality at all.

Before enlightenment, chop wood carry water. After enlightenment chop wood carry water.

No one can return to the eternal realm alone, for the state of mind needed to enter is unity, oneness.

It is this state the ego would have you avoid. But be of good cheer, for as with all things of time and space, there are beginnings and endings.

The ego's days are numbered and it knows it, which lends it to become particularly vicious and cunning once it detects its demise.

The ego would rather see you dead and reincarnate all over again than see you find peace and eternal life.

Without divine assistance however, the demise of the egoist thought system would be a long, long, long way off.

Miracles are real and are your right; you must perform them to see them.

You will see them when you believe in them.

No one gets into heaven through dying. Death is the result of refusal to relinquish egoist thinking.

Think clearly, would you allow a mass murderer into a childcare center, for such the ego is, and every mind on earth has one, uses one and happily endorses their egoist actions in the name of love.

Yet Love **eternal** and **unconditional,** awaits us all when we choose to finally put away our self-righteousness and forgive our neighbors, *our* illusions. And like it or not, it will only be through complete purification of the mind of all egoist thought processes, that the mind can finally reintegrate into a constancy of eternal awareness, where it actually already is.

God is indeed calling you home and does not judge, yet to pass through the gates of heaven you must be checked at the door, no mementos of your earthly journey allowed. Heaven is a holy state of mind, not even the cleanest of thoughts can compare to anything from heaven. A snowflake in heaven would be like an oil slick across the Caribbean. No souvenirs…

So on to some new ideas, or perhaps they are not so new to you and are merely reminders. I have put these up front for impact value. I don't expect you will believe them at first. That's okay neither did I . . . at first.

There's no real way to ease into it so . . . buckle your seatbelt Dorothy. Kansas is going "bye bye".

Physical existence is a dream, an illusion to keep the mind convinced that it is that which it is not . . . a body.

The physical realm is a self-imposed prison sentence designed for one purpose, the attempted destruction of God.

Accept it or not, it is the truth.

Each of us has willingly chosen to use the power of our free will in an attempt to usurp the throne of God by casting ourselves into a dream, in a pitiful attempt to convince ourselves into believing we are separate from God, each other and every living thing.

Yet the one law, which cannot be avoided or denied, is that *all is one*. Eventually every mind will come to learn that *even in the physical realm*, the laws serving the greater good always comes first, and that each of us is a part of a whole.

The purpose governing the discernment of just what the greater good in the physical realm is, though, highly unstable and open to two perspectives, yet death, (that of the ego), will always be illusory.

Love, (of your true eternal Self), will always be true. Yet whilst your allegiance waivers, truth must wait.

The law of free will deems that you have complete freedom of choice as to from whose table you will dine. But you cannot eat from both; it is impossible to attain life and death as one cancels out the other.

If eternal life is real, then there can be no death anyway . . . except in an illusion or a dream.

But an illusion or dream is not reality, and reality does not conquer unreality. It could not even know of an opposite since it is all that is real. It merely waits for the dreamer to awaken.

Exactly like a dream at night, the outside world does not even know that you are asleep and dreaming. It just goes on regardless. You can awake and join in or not.

But no one can be asleep and awake at the same time.

Brief experiences/glimpses (holy instants) of the eternal state and or direct and complete temporary union (enlightenment) with God can indeed be earned through deep devotion, yet the non-necessity to repeat yet another physical sojourn cannot be reached without full purification.

The goal can indeed be experienced and must. Yet the means are still needed to reach it.

This can indeed take many lifetimes, or perhaps simply many miracles, depending on the choices each mind makes for its progress. Each mind's journey is different in this regard but it is the same in that time winds slowly on uncaringly regardless.

It is possible for the mind to reach a satisfactory state of peace quite quickly, and begin having experiences, which will enhance and invigorate the student to further collaborative participation. However having experiences is not the sign of accomplishment. Remembering God is.

No universe, no world, no body, no perception, no realms nor light beings or angels, no observer, no observed...only the oneness of God; I in He and He in Me.

Unconditional Love

Think of your mind as a ball of light, clean and untainted by judgment, grievance and desires. This is how God sees you, innocent and perfect as He/It created you.

Now . . . How do you see you? How do you see others? Are you beginning to get the picture? Well it goes much deeper than that.

There are some sweet minds I've met who tell me they do not

have an ego. This is of course impossible since having an ego is the prerequisite to being in the dream of time and space and maintaining a physical body.

It is the ego's delight that we think of ourselves as good and loving and nice and live in spiritually based denial/ignorance of what lurks beneath the happy façade; pain, misery, murderous rage and death.

Until the dark side of our temporal nature is exposed and admitted to and healed and our nice, sweet side brought down off its pedestal, leaving us humbled and grounded, no gains can really be made towards the goal.

We tend to simply circle about on one foot, with the other spiked to the ground, living in a king of quasi spirituality which eventually sees us work our way into a deep rut of hollowness and emptiness until our ankle snaps and we eventually cry out for help from our gully of midlife crisis, cancer, Alzheimer's or stroke etc.

There is no one special here. We are all sinners and saints both in this realm. But luckily we are not really in this realm, and can shed our false self-identities as easily as we adopted them.

This story then is about just that – the shedding of the self-identities I made for myself to distract myself from the painful admission that I had absolutely no clue who I was, what I was doing here or what here even was.

Those who have not experienced the awesome unspeakable nature of direct union with God cannot possibly imagine what wonder and beauty this world holds.

Beyond every illusory form, the Holy one peeps out saying gently, "Here I am child".

To be satisfied with concepts of God or imagining about God is to be satisfied with a coffin. Only the direct experience of going beyond the body and the physical realm entirely, into the formlessness of God is anything at all.

Everything else is nothing, and does not exist.

To reach enlightenment is to attain liberation from the physical realm of suffering and death. The ticket home to the reality which no one has ever really left, wherein each man actually still is, but believes he is not, Heaven.

All form is illusory. A vast deception, given the illusion of authenticity by the senses, those receptive devices serving the part of the mind which believes it is separate from the whole, taught by its own free will, of its own imaginary teacher that is often called Satan, yet which in modern understanding is more simply understood as the ego.

Like the world in which it would have man believe, the ego also is but an illusion, for no opposite to god can actually exist at all.

God is all encompassing, without opposite forever, perfect, and of God all that is created is the same . . . One.

Even in this world the law of love can be realized or understood, for although through enormous effort man tries deliberately to avoid his reality, it is ultimately and thankful impossible.

Eventually the time must come for every mind to question its reality in this world, for although the threshold for pain and suffering can be quite high, it is not without limit, and each will come to question within themselves that there must be a better way.

This is the beginning of the end for the ego, for although allegiance to it may still be held in ignorance and arrogance, it is no longer seen as wholly desirable, and a space has been made in the mind, an opening, into which light, (reason), can enter.

From this point on the ego will employ all manner of subtle and cunning tactics to re-attract man's allegiance and without support man will very likely easily lose his way yet again, and slip into conflict and madness once more.

Yet as with before, ultimately he will abandon the ego entirely simply because pain is intolerable and because the call to awaken is universal and unending as long as any man anywhere believes he is what he is not . . . a body.

Man is truly blind and deaf. He sees what does not exist, and hears what is silent. And all around him the Universe as God created it, sings to him in glorious unending harmony, calling him to breathe of the air of Creation, his real Home.

Everything that appears to be man's world reflects all the gifts of spirit all the time. It calls ceaselessly to him reminding him, (and I am referring to him/man, as the species), that he is not from this realm and can never find rest here.

Yet buried deep in its introverted existence man denies what is, and ardently employs the power of free will to maintain a level of vibration that is not a lot less dense than lead, purely and simply because it is afraid of the power of its own thinking.

And the reason for this is that the very first experience of change, 'the separation' or the descent into form, was man's first experience of the power of its mind, in a mis-creative way.

Man has been fearful of repeating this error ever since, and so, it falsely believes that to deny the responsibility for its thoughts is a safe and sure protection against further disaster. Man's concept of 'victimization' is a clear example of this erroneous thought process.

In its cellular makeup man carries the blueprint of every single thought, and event that has occurred throughout all of time, and he knows it! He also carries within that same blueprint the correction for all error past and every inevitability still to come, which in linear terms may span many billions of years, and entail that 'man' reincarnate itself many other worlds.

Yet throughout the entire dream realm, man is never comfortless.

At any single instant man may turn within for a true purpose and discover what he has denied, and surrender to it.

Initially this will be attempted under man's own terms, which denies the very concept of surrender actually.

Religion is such an attempt: to seek God in format or ritual.

Many, many years or perhaps lifetimes may be spent bound in religiosity, declaring surrender to divine will and practicing devotional acts as a display to himself that he has surrendered. Yet until man has indeed experienced Oneness, he has not surrendered even one inch.

God is forever willing to give everything unconditionally to man for the simple asking, yet so long as man asks under its own terms which are egoic separation devices, he will never know God nor the creation from which he sprang.

Whilst man is not willing to receive the memory of unconditional reality in its wholeness, he cannot receive it at all.

And he is actually actively choosing yet another death episode in favor of eternality.

The spiritual identity is the loftiest and highest self-identity of which the ego can allow man to reach, beyond this ego cannot go and it knows it.

It will employ all its arsenal at this point to keep man firmly and erroneously fixed in the belief that it has found God.

Yet beliefs are always subject to change, and in fact are entirely understood as meaningless once Self-realization has dawned upon the mind.

Man, a creature of leisure by nature, will feel good at this level since this level carries such enlightening concepts that allow man to think it has arrived as far as it can or need go, and in a sense this is indeed true.

However at *any* point in man's 'journey', he can decide for himself the very same thing. God sets no criteria for man's surrender, no levels of worthiness, nor agenda of any sort.

God simply is.

Thus, the highest conceptual frequency of thought man can entertain of God, also is the gateway to man's freedom, very literally the door to heaven.

Yet a door is not the end of the journey. What's on the other side is. And so man will bounce up against this door for as long as he feels he can avoid the inevitable, in a false belief that he can easily enter heaven now that he knows where the door is.

Still is surrender on his own terms, and conceptual, rather than abstract thought.

It is that man must be wholly willing to abandon egoic premise, and desire only God and be willing to leave behind even that desire to simply accept God . . . as it is.

It is a curious thing that man should entertain the idea of God as being in man's likeness in any way at all, especially when man is subject even unto the rigors of evolution, yet holds that God is Spirit and changeless.

How strange that man should think God knows about man at all. God knows only itself, and 'knows' in this sense is perhaps better understood if it is seen as a relationship rather than an understanding.

God is eternally God, the Creator and Creation forever. A force that pervades even mortal life, unseen yet more real than the air man believes he is breathing.

God must be met entirely on its own terms, which of course is unconditionally. The one term that has no terms at all.

Each member of the species of man is what God is, as co-creator, imbued equally with creative will, as creative will.

The entirety of the 'family' of man, is what in Christian terminology referred to as the Christ.

This is the extension of God, as unconditional Love . . . Light.

Let there be light!

Man can indeed choose to think of itself other than this and identify itself with its learning device which it calls its body. Yet it cannot ever truly be anything other than Spirit because there is no separation . . . only a dream into which man has wandered.

Yet creation goes on all around him, unseen deliberately and fearfully denied. As a man thinks, so it shall be for him, for such is the power of thought . . . God.

Ever since the advent of the resurrection of Christ, the whole continuum of reality man identifies as time and space, has been subtly and continually collapsing.

The insertion of reason (light) brought forth through the man known as Jesus, (and indeed many others who also carried his message), has slowly been expanding. Having been taken on board by man, it is pervading his consciousness, allowing him to increasingly become aware of factors and happenings beyond himself and the little universe of death in which he has imprisoned himself.

The very denial of death, demonstrated by the resurrection has undermined the one certainty upon which man has erroneously placed his faith, that being of course, that all things die.

Man has depended upon death as an end to his suffering over and over. Yet even though God is a known certainty within him, man has insisted that death also must be true, since, like God, death can only be experienced.

However unlike God, death is not eternal, and man must undergo yet more trials in the physical realm, incarnating over and over until finally death is seen and accepted for what it truly is, an illusion.

The plan for the teachers is part of the Atonement principle, brought into accord and motion for man to begin to enter into a new frequency of thought; one which is stable and reflects singularity in its undertaking.

The plan for Atonement was formed long before the resurrection, yet the resurrection is the symbol for the plan.

The resurrection established the entry and permanence of a 'portal' of light energy that literally resonates as heaven on earth, yet cannot be used on earth for any other purpose other than to allow more and more individuals of the species to enter into accord with it, and stay true to it, for the purpose of becoming 'miracle mined', so as to collapse time.

The true use of time is to realize that time itself is unnecessary so as to enable man to accept atonement and regain knowledge.

ALL attempts to use spiritual power for worldly gain or purpose are egoic efforts at destruction, and many are misguided in their attempts to do so.

Many falsely believe they are helping things by doing this and many religions and healing practices are examples of this.

Each has at its core a true desire to heal, yet each fails to accept that only salvation can heal in its entirety and that is always of God.

The time will, and now is come when man must look squarely at the cause of death within himself individually and see that there is actually no cause at all, healing symptoms is merely a delaying strategy of the ego.

Man must, will and did learn to think miraculously, and return his mind to God as it was given him . . . unconditionally.

Attempting to establish an empire or existence in this physical realm will never succeed and using spiritual excuses for the attempt to do so is the highest excuse of the ego, and also ends in death.

Any time man believes that the course of even one minute is up to his direction he is bound to death.

Man has no idea what he is, where he is going or where he came from. How curious then that he would attempt to plan his life or set any goals other than the source of knowledge.

How curious that he believes he knows what is best for him.

I tell you the sounds of the laughter of angels, rings loudly in man's ears, even now, and man could hear this laughter if only he were wholly willing to join in and laugh himself.

I could not end this writing without that I recommend and remind mankind of the availability of the offering to train himself to become miracle minded quickly and thoroughly, through the availability of the divine teachings and workbook of 'A Course in Miracles'.

There are many 'paths' to God that point the way equally well. This one is simply the one that was presented to me upon my 'return' to this realm from reality. It is the most complete and most contemporary modality for mind transformation to date.

Those of the species who might like to undertake a 'speedup' of their own process of awakening would do well to be vigilant for this course and its practical application in their daily lives. It is my personal instruction from its author that it is the fastest aid in bringing man to his own individual surrender to date.

Work is being carried out on an awakening pill, designed to indeed disrupt man's inverse carrier signal, much like in the film, 'The Matrix'.

Due to the obvious one off nature of such a pills application, this may not be a marketable/viable product for some time to come.

Even if it were, mind training would still be required to stabilize the experience.

It is strongly advised then that time is indeed of the essence. Delay or tardiness to commitment should be avoided as much as possible.

Your salvation process is up to you, your surrender is not. No one else can awaken you. The delight and freedom that comes from letting go of fear and realizing God are each man's inheritance to be claimed . . . Here and Now.

To study ego validates its existence . . . to concentrate on error is what error is.

All pain comes from attachment to observance of temporal cause and effect relationships.

Yet through these relationships, truth will be discerned.

Release from suffering is impossible . . . Suffering does not exist.

The idea of Liberation is its own time making circle . . . you are already free.

GOD IS!

POETRY

INTRODUCTION

The meaning and lessons behind these poems will be revealed in full as you undergo changes to your consciousness through the steps of your arranged spiritual journey.

On the surface they may appear whimsical and notion-less poetry but to the learned student of spirituality they will convey deeper meanings over the years as the individual's progress and understanding deepens.

These poems all came through in one period of about 6 months in total wherein I would undergo long weeks and months of sleeplessness and would be drawn to the office at the spiritual centre where I lived to type them out as inspired.

I would often find with writing most of this stuff that it would come to me late at night in a moment of quiet, often accompanied by sleeplessness and restlessness.

At times I often felt like I wanted to crawl out of my skin and that I could not stand being in my physical body I discovered that a very hot bath or writing in this way often helped to alleviate the symptoms of spiritual transformation that I was experiencing at the time.

Enjoy!

As you run from me, yet you run to me,
Though your way may be troubled and pained.
For there's nowhere you can run but through me,
Yet in dreams do you think you can gain.

So I give you your dream whilst you want it,
Though I know you are happier at home,
So if one day you stop and turn to me,
I'll show you the way you should roam.

For the world holds out naught but illusions,
And you see them wherever you go,
Yet in each is my hand held out through them,
Just take it and love will you know.

For in this one who now stands before you,
I AM,
Beyond sickness or health,
For its you that you'll see,
Your reflection,
In the one choice for death,
Or the Self.

Can any man hear of the winds gentle voice,
To the seed of the grass on the plains?.
There is no need, yet I speak it to you now.

Or can any man know of the love of his enemies
For their children's hopes?.
He cannot, yet I show you of it now.

For all men are deaf as are all of men blind,
And none who but comes to dwell herein
Shall not live in his filth as is his need.

His heart's desire remains bound to his freedom,
And by his ignorance is he dead already,
Enslaved to the darkness.

Cast away, ye lubber lads, from sea and from the land,
Then cast away ye lubber ways,
Of greedy wants and selfish hands.

Oh cast away yer lubber lungs that draw yer stinking breath,
To fill the world with words untrue,
And draw ye to yer death.

Yae come about a compass turn, and face into the wind,
To set yer sights for heavens shores, and seek the light within.

Dear child,
Those flowers in your hair,
Once graced my feet as I skipped with the wind,
Across these meadows, 2000 year ago, just now ago,
Wild days, born to be wild, no longer angry, just wild,
Like a just busted virgin, a teenage screamer who's got it all,
Like so many fuzzy good feelings that sneak in
When we let ourselves expand
With the song of love, wild and free.

Tell someone of the joy of it all, please, write it in paint,
Play it on your drum, even if they cannot hear, I will hear,
Your chorus spreading abstract seeds, falling willy nilly
From your tussled hair and clothes,

I came for you once but you were not ready,
But now I can see that the shackles are off,
You laugh for no reason,
This world rejects you, wants to be rid of you,
I see you have no friends in the world . . .
Good, good . . .

There is a great wedding party for you to attend,
A divine old
Drunk is waiting to give you away,
To the universe . . .

Forget not, to laugh, this life is a dream.
A pitiful nightmare that keeps truth unseen.
Question the riddle that dodges your mind,
Among twisted perversions you can seem to find.

It's hidden within like a sliver of glass,
A lifetime to find it, or kiss you own ass.
Today or tomorrow, but now must you look,
As time passes by you're the bait and the hook.

In one single instant the truth will you find,
But not whilst you quest in the worlds of the blind.
Step out of your smug supercilious grin,
You are your own jailer stop trying to win.

You are an illusion, I've told you before,
I called you to seek and to knock on the door.
I know that you doubt me, you trust your own flaws,
That lead you on grimly to the death you adore.

Yet go with my blessing to what you may find,
That ole' casket of wood, or freedom of mind.
Asleep or awake it's all up to you,
But it's over I tell you, now what will you do?

The final frontier, you so frantically sought,
Was not in your concepts, but simply in thought.

I can draw no maps for love,
For of a field of wheat,
There is no memory of the harvest.
Nor, to the goings of oceans,
Do their islands raise question.

Yet who finds a stranger is lost indeed,
In time's merciless grip,
Questioning memories,
Adrift among the harvest of serenity,
In the torment of a nightmare,
Asleep.

I jig a little this way,
And trip a little that,
A drinking of the spirit,
I grow a little fat.

A hearty laugh I bellow,
A titter or tee hee,
I'm eating of the bread again,
Come break a bit with me.

A tipping hat, a welcome mat,
A smiley howdy doo,
I'm all a glow because I know,
We're all a golden hue.

A dotty little ditty,
I sing just 'cause I might,
Lay down at last this body past,
And blip into the light.

I love you more than all the twinkles
Any realm of stars has ever twunk,
In heights higher than any mountain peak,
In depths deeper than the greatest ocean abyss.

My love for you is greater than the greatest of the sun's rays,
More inviting than a new spring morning.

If every butterfly ever hatched in all of time
Flapped its wings for all of time,
Not even the beautiful gale of winds they made
Would be more than a puff in compare to
The grandeur of the tempest of my mighty love.

Today, 80 000 people cheered for an hour,
And partied all night,
For their winning soccer team.

Such a celebration is but a tear in the ocean of forever
That is constantly in joyous delight,
At the thought of you I hold.

Should every artist and poet ever born,
Every musician and bard ever that roamed the world,
Sit in repose a million years,
To create tribute to your holiness,
They could not make even one mark of composition
To capture your eternal essence.

For beyond that vessel of skins,
I know you are the glint from the smile of the Lord,
And my words fail utterly to say how much I love you.

Yet nothing in the whole universe
Is more worthy of my attempt.

Oh the times are changing,
I'm certain my friend,
The signs in the sky have abandoned their trend.

The grass is all brown,
From an absence of rain,
The cosmic attunement is humming again.

The call to stay faithful,
Not wander in doubt,
Is certainly felt . . . Isaiah's about.

Temptation to scatter,
To stray from the flock,
I hear resound loud though my sanctum unlocked.

Oh hail ye my brothers,
Raise staff and hand high,
And stand together lest wandering ye die.

For Christ is the shepherd,
Through drought and through rain,
He's leading us home, let him not lead in vain.

Ole Whore's Bed
September 9, 2011 at 8:05am

Thanks all you holy rollers, you freaks and fuckers too
Cheers for all the crap and fun, that for a while seemed true,
But now I've taken all my senses, and stuck 'em in a box
Put 'em 'neath an ole whore's bed,
where they can catch the pox.

So next time when you see me, don't act all on the stage
That script is done, our hearts are one, we're on the final page
There's no fat lady singing, no icicles in hell
Only peace and quiet now, far from the body's smell.

So let's sit here and share a beer, whilst time still seems to last
And wait for those last stragglers, we left in acts gone past
They'll be here any moment, with feint scars from the locks
That I once applied to make God cry,
back then when I was lost.

So hooray for brother Jesus, who turned the water red
And led me to a living death, beneath an ole whore's bed.
This moment is so everything, a wild eternity
If you're not sure I'm speaking truth, crawl under here and see...

Ollie Ollie Wicktenstein,
Fell asleep and dreamed a dream,
Sailed adrift upon a yacht built of lies and doomed to rot,
Ran around upon beliefs
That sunk him deep,
And in his grief,
Laughed aloud with open eyes
That bobbed about from side to side,
Almost the loudest laugh you've heard,
Then Ollie turned into a bird,
But under water could not fly,
So Ollie Ollie drowned and died.

The Blanket Theatre

Here in the deep sleep of the blanket theatre are all of us actors,
I am the cast,
without question,
The boss, the employee,
The parent, the judge,
The juror, the teacher,
The student, the architect,
The soldier, the corpse,
The clown, the politician,
The taxi driver, the poet,
The artist, the alcoholic,
The widow, the bride,
The victims one and all,
As the world turns,
They are born and they die.

To make a mark, or not,
Upon the walls of their prison.
Among them,
I am holding out the golden chalice they seek
For the toils of their Performances.

Yet they do not take it.
For fear it denies them applause
In the theatre of
Dreams.

The Deceiver

Come tarry a while,
And I'll play you a tune,
Where the moon maidens dance
And the dream weavers swoon.

Give over your bodies,
In me put your trust,
I'll nurture your hatred
And fill you with lust,

Submit to my treasures,
Come stay on the wheel,
Consider my offer,
A most gracious deal.

Creation won't miss you,
A few lifetimes more,
Come share my oasis,
Don't knock on that door.

What fun would you have,
Without trouble and strife,
Consider the boredom
Of eternal life,

So listen I beg thee,
Come under my spell,
I'll speak you of love
(Whilst I keep you in hell.)

The pool of miscreation is crowded now,
The whole world paddles meaninglessly about in its shallows,
Running inevitably out of the room.

Many of its number are forced to the depths,
Unwilling they go,
To certainly drown.

There are a few, individuals,
who abandoning . . . un,
Will to go,
These ones do not drown,
And diving into the unknown,
Discover not the fathomless depths,
But the memory of swimming like a fish . . .
Forever.

It's very much a cardboard cutout sort of day,
The theatre of mind begins its nothing doings,
In very much a nothing doing way.

A cameo appearance by some apparently aimless tourists,
I take this costume to the shower room . . .
Ta Da,
The star.

I'm toddling down the mountain,
My tablets, stone, in hand,
Through rosy cheeks my laughter peeps,
God's prophet, in this land.

To carry to the people,
Commandments that are hewn,
To stand in time and realign
The wayward and the new.

Yet toddling in excitement,
Entrusted with these plates,
I tripped across a sprig of vines,
And crumbled 'neath their weight.

Oh blast the task I've taken,
To carry all fifteen,
I have now failed, yet ten prevail,
Perhaps I've not been seen.

Oh curse my roman sandals made,
That set me in a rush,
Israeli shoes would never lose their grip
In spriggy brush.

Forgive me lord, my silly ways,
That see me buying shoes
That cannot toddle, falling flat,
No wonder Rome will lose.

What will you give, o man,
That I may pull your own sword from your heart,
That you may finally die to your one idea,
That you may no longer taste the soils embrace,
The bite of the worm,
Or the sear of the flames at your bones

Oh what will you give, oh man,
To be given from slave hood,
Unto the service of life.

Will you give, in this whole world,
Even one small room,
Within which I may come,
To live in an among you.?

For should even one among you offer it
144,000 will rise up in your service,
To pave the way before you,
In fields of gold.

This book could continue on for many chapters to come but that would only be a repetitive exercise and necessitate a greater letting of conceptual thought processes down the track.

Seek for the door and find it!

Amen

Thank You Father

The Author of this manuscript lives in Australia.

He can be contacted via email at:
tattmonktoo@live.com.au
Mobile: 61+ 0401 442 200

Lightning Source UK Ltd.
Milton Keynes UK
UKHW010658231122
412659UK00001B/379

9 780646 955025